revision guides

KT-436-795

Do**Brilliantly**

GCSE English

Exam practice at its **best**

■ **Andrew Bennett**

■ **Series Editor: Jayne de Courcy**

Published by HarperCollins*Publishers* Ltd
77-85 Fulham Palace Road
London W6 8JB

www.**Collins**Education.com
On-line support for schools and colleges

First published 2001
This edition 2003
10 9 8 7 6 5 4 3 2
ISBN 0 00 714856 9

Andrew Bennett asserts the moral right to be identified as the author of this work.

British Library Cataloguing in Publication Data
A catalogue record for this book is available from the British Library.

Edited by Sue Chapple
Production by Jack Murphy
Book design by Gecko Ltd
Printed and bound in China by Imago.

Acknowledgements
The Author and Publishers are grateful to the following for permission to
reproduce copyright material:

Faber and Faber for *The Early Purges* from *Opened Ground* by Seamus Heaney;
Scholastic Ltd for the extract from *Designer Genes* by Phil Gates; also to the
following Exam Boards for permission to reproduce GCSE questions: CCEA
(pp 9, 65-7, 77); London Examinations, a division of Edexcel Foundation (pp 35-6,
56, 60, 72); AQA (NEAB) (pp 48, 50, 54, 60, 74-6, 78 Question 2); OCR (pp 26-7, 42,
44, 68-70, 78 Question 3); WJEC (pp 7, 20, 29-30, 73-4).

Answers to questions taken from past examination papers, and all commentaries,
are entirely the responsibility of the author and have neither been provided nor
approved by any of the above organisations.

Illustrations
Cartoon artwork – Dave Mostyn

You might also like to visit:
www.**fire**and**water**.com
The book lover's website

Contents

How this book will help you

by Andrew Bennett

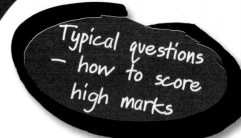

Typical questions – how to score high marks

This book takes you through the different kinds of Reading and Writing questions you will come across in your English exam papers. It helps you **identify key words in questions and revise key skills in answering questions**. It makes clear what examiners look for in answers in order to award them high marks.

Reading through this book as part of your revision will **help you with your exam technique and give you the best possible chance of achieving a high grade in your exam**.

The first nine chapters in this book are broken down into five elements aimed at giving you as much guidance as possible:

❶ Typical exam questions

Each chapter contains **two typical exam questions, selected from different exam boards**. For Reading, these are usually part questions, so that they don't take up too much space. For Writing, they are usually complete questions. **I have emphasised and commented on the key words in these questions**. This should help you to understand clearly what is required by the questions which you meet in your exam. So often students lose marks in their exam because they misread or misinterpret the questions.

❷ Extracts from students' answers at Grade C and Grade A

I have chosen extracts from a **Grade C** answer to the first exam question. **I highlight the good points and then show how you could score higher marks**. I have chosen extracts from a **Grade A** answer to the second exam question. Here **I make clear what makes this such a good answer so that you can try to demonstrate similar skills in your own exam answers**. I have used **extracts** rather than complete answers so that you can immediately see the points which are being made and don't have too much to read!

❸ 'Don't forget...' boxes

These boxes highlight **all the really important things you need to remember** when tackling a particular type of Reading or Writing question in your exam. You might like to read these boxes through the night before your exam as a 'quick check' on what to do to score high marks.

❹ Key skill

This section focuses on a **key Reading or Writing skill**. I have written it as **a series of easy-to-remember bullet points** so that you can simply and quickly revise what you have learnt during your English course.

❺ What the examiners are looking for

This page tells you as clearly as possible what an examiner expects from an answer in order to award it a Grade C or a Grade A. **This should help you to demonstrate 'high scoring' skills in your answers to exam questions**.

Practice questions, answers and examiner's comments

Chapters 10 and 11 contain **actual Reading and Writing exam questions which I have selected from across different exam boards**. These questions are for you to try answering once you have read through the earlier chapters.

You can use these practice questions in different ways. For example:

- Read the question and then go straight to the model answer, trying to identify what is good about it.
- Try writing your own answers to some of the questions and then compare them with the model answers given, to see what you might have done differently, or better.

Sometimes, **it is a good idea to give yourself a time limit when answering questions**, so that you are used to being under this kind of pressure before you sit the actual exam.

When you attempt these questions for yourself, and when you look at the model answers, **think carefully about how you need to shape a whole answer** – how the sequence of ideas has to be logical and coherent, how the response has to be opened and closed so that the examiner understands what you are doing, and is interested in your ideas and the way you express them.

Exam Tips

- **Read the Chief Examiner's report on previous exams**: so that you know why answers succeed or fail generally, and the common mistakes candidates make.
- **Study past papers**: so that you are unlikely to be surprised by the style of questions you see in the exam.
- **Study mark schemes for past papers**: so that you know how marks are gained in specific types of questions.
- **Practise writing to the time limits of the exam**: so that you can write neatly and accurately at speed.
- **Prepare and annotate pre-release materials thoroughly**.
- **Read all instructions on the paper carefully** so that you can:
  - be sure how many questions you have to answer;
  - work out how long to spend on each question.
- **Study the questions carefully**:
  - look at key words so that you understand exactly what you have to do;
  - note any advice about structuring your answer – for example, there may be a series of bullet points or headings to follow.
- **Plan your answers** in note or outline form, to make sure that you:
  - don't rush into answers before you have thought through all that you want to say;
  - can think about the overall shape and logic of your answer;
  - choose the best references to texts in Reading questions.
- **Check your answers**, so that you know you have:
  - expressed yourself clearly;
  - used accurate spelling, punctuation and grammar;
  - included relevant material and ideas;
  - used references and quotations where necessary.

All the exam groups in England, Wales and Northern Ireland have to set exam questions which cover certain core Reading and Writing skills. This means that although different kinds of papers and questions are set by each Exam Board, **everything you revise by using this book will be valuable to you somewhere in your exam.**

How this book matches your exam board's requirements

So that you can focus first on the sections which relate directly to your exam group's papers, this chart shows you where there are direct links. The numbers across the top refer to the numbered chapters in this book, and the information down the left-hand side details the exam papers set by the different groups.

Group	Paper	1	2	3	4	5	6	7	8	9	10	11	12	13	14
AQA (NEAB)	1F/H		✓		✓				✓		✓	✓	✓	✓	✓
	2F/H	✓						✓			✓	✓	✓	✓	✓
AQA (SEG)	5/7			✓	✓	✓			✓		✓	✓	✓	✓	✓
	6/8	✓	✓						✓	✓	✓	✓	✓	✓	✓
EDEXCEL	2F/4H		✓	✓				✓			✓	✓	✓	✓	✓
	3F/5H				✓	✓			✓	✓	✓	✓	✓	✓	✓
OCR	1F/3H			✓	✓	✓			✓		✓	✓	✓	✓	✓
	2F/4H	✓					✓	✓			✓	✓	✓	✓	✓
WJEC	1F/1H	✓					✓	✓			✓	✓	✓	✓	✓
	2F/2H			✓	✓	✓		✓	✓		✓	✓	✓	✓	✓
CCEA	1F/1H	✓							✓		✓	✓	✓	✓	✓
	2F/2H			✓		✓		✓			✓	✓	✓	✓	✓

Remember that **many skills in Reading and Writing are not easily separated,** and so exam questions will never focus entirely or exclusively on just the areas ticked in the table. Although you will want to concentrate on the skills targeted by your Exam Board in its questions, don't ignore the other sections in this book – they will provide good all-round practice at developing your powers of understanding and expression.

Typical exam question

Read carefully the passage below. Then answer the question which follows it.

It was Sunday. Helen always went to Camden Lock Market on Sunday. As she got ready she sat in front of her enemy, the mirror. She turned her head and looked at herself. Her nose-stud winked. Her parents had been horrified, of course.

"Mutilation!" her Dad had yelled. "My own daughter!"

"Great," Helen had said, smugly.

Trouble was, the three pimples on her chin, they caught the light too. They looked the same size as the nose-stud – no, bigger. *Gigantic*. Oh-why-am-I-alive? She rubbed cream over her horrible face. And why am I so fat? It was Dad's fault; he was pudgy.

What do you learn about Helen in these lines?   [5 marks]

What are the key words in this question?

- *Read carefully* reminds you to look for **details**, not just to make obvious comments.
- It also reminds you to **read between the lines** and think about what effect particular words or phrases have.
- *What do you learn* reminds you that examiners want to read about your own genuine response – there is no 'right answer'.

Grade C answer

Helen is not very happy. She does not like the way she looks because of her spots, which she has to put cream on. She also thinks she is fat. She blames this on her Dad. She is pleased with her nose-stud, and that her parents don't like it.

Good points

UNDERSTANDING: You have realised that Helen has mixed feelings about her appearance, and that there seems to be a problem in her relationship with her parents.

REFERENCES: You have mentioned some important details such as the spots, the cream, the nose-stud, Helen's worry about her size and that she blames her Dad.

How to score higher marks

UNDERSTANDING: You have not shown any 'reading between the lines' or **inference** in your answer. For example, you could have made more of Helen's mixed-up qualities by pointing out that although she has tried to be rebellious by having a nose-stud, she is also very predictable in her habits as she does the same thing every Sunday.

REFERENCES: You could have **quoted and commented** on the word *enemy* which Helen uses to describe the mirror and which sums up her feelings about her own appearance. Another important word is *smugly*, which suggests that Helen was more concerned to upset her parents with the nose-stud than with her appearance.

LANGUAGE AND PRESENTATION: You might have said that the italicised word *Gigantic* and the following phrase *Oh-why-am-I-alive?* suggest that Helen is still quite immature and mixed up because she exaggerates and thinks something serious which she doesn't really mean – the hyphens suggest that she is just repeating it in a mechanical kind of way without thinking what she is really saying. References to *Dad* rather than a more formal word such as *father* suggest that she is in fact quite fond of him.

A better answer

An answer which included the points mentioned would read something like this:

Helen is a mixed-up teenager. She is quite conventional, because she does the same thing every Sunday morning, but she also likes to shock her parents, for example by having a nose-stud. When this made her father yell, she felt smug about his reaction. She is unhappy about her appearance, so much so that she regards her mirror as an enemy. She is immature, because she exaggerates the faults in her appearance, such as her gigantic spots, and her fatness, which she blames on her Dad – but she calls him Dad, not father, which implies she is fond of him, really. She wonders why she is alive, but the way this is written (with hyphens) suggests that she thinks it because she has heard others say it and she hasn't thought through what it actually means.

- This section tests **reading** skills.
- **Read** the passage carefully.
- Answer the question.

Ted looked at him, prepared to tolerate his sister's fancy. He saw immediately that the boy was not the sort to please mothers, being casual and long-haired, and as scruffy as Ruth herself. He was tall and powerfully built, but moved with an arrogant ease; there was a scornful, aggressive air about him that suggested to Ted that he could easily get into trouble, although Ted suspected that not many would want to tangle with him. Ted recognised instantly what it was that attracted Ruth, and no doubt many other girls as well, but to his mother the boy was merely surly and without charm. He did not smile, or say anything at all, ticking off the payment in the book, handing over the loaf, and slouching off with the basket slung over his arm, hands in pockets, shoulders hunched.

Spend **about 9 minutes** on this question. Use **evidence from these lines** to support your answer.

How does the writer suggest that the delivery boy was not a very pleasant or likeable person? [6 marks]

What are the key words in this question?

- The **time** and **mark allocations** give you a clear indication of how long to spend on this question in relation to others on the paper.
- The reference to *evidence* emphasises that the main focus of this question is your ability to **find references** and **use quotations**.
- Note that the question tells you what to think about the delivery boy – you don't have to work this out for yourself!

Grade A answer

The writer uses two methods to suggest that the delivery boy was not very pleasant or likeable. First of all, we see the boy from the viewpoint of three other people: Ted, his sister Ruth, and their mother. Although Ted is wary of the boy, he understands why Ruth has fallen for his similarities to herself in appearance and his air of power and strength, but to their mother the delivery boy is simply unsuitable. The words and phrases used by the writer are the other way of conveying the delivery boy's character: "powerfully built", "arrogant", "scornful" and "aggressive" suggest that he is always ready to pick a fight and that he has a very high opinion of himself. Ted's thought that "he could easily get into trouble" and that "not many would want to tangle with him" make the boy sound quite sinister and dangerous. The mother's description of him as "merely surly and without charm" show that she is more concerned with more superficial social qualities in his character, but she also sees the unpleasant side of him. His lack of response when she buys the loaf reinforces this impression, and the way he "slouches" away with his shoulders "hunched" almost suggests an air of guilt about him, as though he has already done something of which he is ashamed or which he wants to hide.

Why this scores high marks

UNDERSTANDING: You have shown that you understand what the author wants you to feel about the delivery boy, and that this is **achieved in two ways** – how the other three characters react to him, and the language used.

REFERENCES: In talking about the characters' attitudes, you have made **clear references** to what they feel, and why. In talking about the author's language, you have **quoted good examples**.

LANGUAGE AND EFFECTS: You have explained briefly, but in enough detail for this length of answer, why certain words and phrases **convey particular meanings**.

Don't forget ...

The purpose of answering questions about prose texts is to show that you understand the writer's ideas and attitudes and how these are conveyed to the reader.

Questions will usually be about characters who are described, their actions (including what they think, say and do) or the setting of the text.

You will need to identify and describe some of the techniques the writer uses and the effects they have on you, the reader.

There are no right or wrong answers in how you react to a text – the examiner is interested in your own personal response.

You must be able to support what you say by using evidence from the text – this could be a general reference or, better still, an actual quotation.

Even in a test of reading, you must express yourself clearly and logically – the examiner cannot reward answers which are difficult or impossible to understand.

Spend the appropriate amount of time on questions – papers will always tell you how many marks are available for each question, which is a good comparative guide, and will sometimes advise you how long to spend on the answer.

Key skill – reading the question

- The wording of questions should help you read the text, so look at the questions and make sure you **understand what they mean before you read the text**.

- Your **sequence** should be: read **questions** → read **text** → read **questions** again → skim or scan **text** to find information needed in answers → write **answers**, using details from the text as appropriate.

- Look for **key words** in a question:
  - *what* asks you to **describe** something
  - *why* asks you to **explain** something
  - *how* asks you to **identify** the writer's techniques
  - *discuss* asks you to **suggest different meanings or points of view**.

- The key words in the point above are in increasing order of difficulty, so you will gain **more marks for explaining than for describing**; you will gain **very high marks if you can suggest alternative interpretations of a text**, and how the writer's technique contributes to these.

What the examiners are looking for

To achieve a Grade C, your response to reading prose fiction must:

1 Show that you understand what the text is about.

🎯 You must find ways of explaining the obvious, 'surface' meaning and also what is 'between the lines'

2 Show that you can make a personal response to the text.

🎯 Explain what you feel about characters and situations. Do you sympathise with them or not? Do you understand why certain things happen or why people have particular ideas or attitudes?

3 Show that you can comment on aspects of the writer's style, and on the effects it achieves.

🎯 Explain how the writer's choice of words helps you see certain meanings on or below the surface, perhaps through humour or shock, for example.

🎯 Explain how the words or images make you feel about characters and situations. Is there a mix of description and dialogue? If so, does this allow the writer to give you different points of view – and which do you find most sympathetic?

4 Use details from the text effectively.

🎯 You can refer to the text or quote directly from it – preferably the latter.

🎯 You must **use** your references and quotations, in other words by explaining what they show about the character, or the theme, or the writer's use of language.

5 Present your answer clearly and logically.

🎯 The examiner must be able to follow what you are saying.

🎯 You should be putting forward a structured point of view, not just a lot of separate thoughts.

To achieve a Grade A, your response to reading prose fiction must:

1 Show that you can suggest a range of different possible meanings in a text.

🎯 You should speculate and be prepared to be imaginative – but make sure that your suggestions are rooted in textual detail!

2 Analyse how successfully the writer's techniques convey meaning to you.

🎯 You should be confident in making judgements, for example about how and why you do or do not like the way the writer has chosen certain adjectives or has made a character speak in a particular way.

3 Relate details in the text to each other.

🎯 You must show that you can take in the whole text, for example by linking something at the end to something near the beginning, rather than just working through it from beginning to end.

4 Integrate references and quotations into your answer.

🎯 You should try not always to set out quotations or references separately, but to make them flow into your writing by including them within sentences.

5 Develop and sustain your answer.

🎯 You must develop the main points of your answer in considerable detail and link your ideas into a convincing and original overall approach.

🎯 You must present a logical and coherent point of view, and not contradict yourself.

Read carefully the following poem.

The Early Purges

I was six when I first saw kittens drown.
Dan Taggart pitched them, "the scraggy wee shits",
Into a bucket; a frail metal sound

Soft paws scraping like mad. But their tiny din
Was soon soused. They were slung on the snout
Of the pump and the water pumped in.

"Sure isn't it better for them now?" Dan said.
Like wet gloves they bobbed and shone till he sluiced
Them out on the dunghill, glossy and dead.

Suddenly frightened, for days I sadly hung
Round the yard, watching the three sogged remains
Turn mealy and crisp as old summer dung

Until I forgot them. But the fear came back
When Dan trapped big rats, snared rabbits, shot crows
Or, with a sickening tug, pulled old hens' necks.

Still, living displaces false sentiments
And now, when shrill pups are prodded to drown
I just shrug, "Bloody pups". It makes sense:

"Prevention of cruelty" talk cuts ice in town
Where they consider death unnatural,
But on well-run farms pests have to be kept down.

Seamus Heaney

How does the poet bring out the thoughts of an adult remembering childhood experiences?
You should write about:

● the child's thoughts and feelings
● the adults' thoughts and feelings
● how Heaney uses language to bring out those thoughts and feelings.

What are the key words in this question?

● *How* is the most important word here: this tells you not just to rewrite the story of what happens in the poem but to **explain the ways in which the poet has an effect on his readers.**

● *Thoughts and feelings* again reminds you not to spend too much time describing events, but rather the reactions they cause in the minds of the *child* and the *adults*. (Note the important **position of the apostrophe** in the question: this signals to you that you need to write about both Dan Taggart and the poet when he has grown up.)

● Finally, you are told to approach this question by writing about the *language* Heaney uses.

Grade C answer

The child thinks it is very cruel when the kittens are killed because he doesn't like to see them being drowned and then thrown onto a rubbish heap. He feels very sad when he hears them trying to escape from the bucket and he stays upset for some time afterwards.

Dan Taggart isn't bothered about killing animals because it is his job to keep the farm clear of pests. When the poet is grown up he also realises this and thinks that people who live in towns shouldn't be so silly about killing animals.

The poet uses some good language to bring out these thoughts and feelings. When the boy says the drowned kittens looked like "wet gloves" it makes you see them through the child's eyes, but to Dan they are just "scraggy wee shits". When the poet has grown up he uses similar language ("Bloody pups") and agrees that "on well-run farms pests have to be kept down".

How to score higher marks

UNDERSTANDING: You need to **read between the lines** of the poem more – the poet was upset by the drowned kittens, but then he "forgot" them; is he really so hardened to it now, or is the last line of the poem just big talk?

STRUCTURE: You should try to **integrate** different aspects of the answer. In other words, don't deal with the bullet points one after another, but build your references to language into your comments on the people, and try to contrast the child's views with the adults' rather than treating them separately.

An answer which included the points mentioned would read something like this:

The poet is at first upset and frightened by what he sees Dan Taggart do. He doesn't like to hear the "soft paws scraping" on the bucket — the 's' sound itself is soft, and the word "scraping" is onomatopoeic, so we can sense the child's feelings towards the desperate kittens and towards the hard Dan Taggart, to whom they are just "scraggy wee shits", a succession of harsh, dismissive sounds. When the dead kittens seem like "wet gloves" to the child, the choice of words creates a convincing child's-eye picture, because he probably had to wear black woollen gloves in cold weather.

However, the child does eventually forget the kittens, but is reminded of his fears when Dan kills other animals, for example strangling old hens "with a sickening tug" of their necks; again, the word "tug" is short and nasty like the action it describes and the feeling it brings about in the child. In the final two stanzas, we are not quite sure of the grown-up poet's attitude. He sounds more like Dan now in his use of swear words ("Bloody pups") and in his attitude about "pests" on farms. But his thoughts are very unemotional and he may be putting on an act to make it seem as though he doesn't care any more — when he says "living displaces false sentiments" it sounds too easy to be completely convincing. But we don't really know!

Read carefully the following poem.

The Voice

Woman much missed, how you call to me, call to me,
Saying that now you are not as you were
When you had changed from the one who was all to me,
But as at first, when our day was fair.

Can it be you that I hear? Let me view you, then,
Standing as when I drew near to the town
Where you would wait for me: yes, as I knew you then,
Even to the original air-blue gown!

Or is it only the breeze, in its listlessness
Travelling across the wet mead to me here,
You being ever dissolved to wan wistlessness
Heard no more again far or near?

    Thus I; faltering forward,
    Leaves around me falling,
Wind oozing thin through the thorn from norward,
    And the woman calling.

Thomas Hardy

How does Hardy convey his sense of loss in this poem?
Support your answer with examples of how he uses language.

What are the key words in this question?

- *How* is again the vital word, so you must **explain** what is going on in the poem, not merely describe it.
- *Loss* gives you a strong clue about how to interpret the poem, so you don't have to worry about searching for other meanings.
- How Hardy *uses language* gives you the focus for your answer.

Grade A answer

In this poem, Hardy conveys his sense of loss through describing a strange experience when he believes he can hear the voice of a woman who is not with him any more. In a way, he describes a double loss, because first the woman changed from how she had been when they fell in love, and then she went away – or perhaps died – and the poet feels guilty that their relationship had deteriorated before this, and now is over for ever.

On one level, then, Hardy conveys his sense of loss by describing how he thinks (and wishes) he can hear the woman, but it is only an illusion. The repeated "call to me" in the first line represents the repeated sounds he hears which he thinks at first are the woman speaking but later realises are "the wind oozing thin through the thorn from norward"; in this line, the repeated 'th' sounds echo the empty noise of the wind and contrast it with the voice of the loved-one he had hoped it would be. His reference to the "air-blue gown" also symbolises a happy earlier relationship through association with beautiful summer skies.

On the second level, Hardy remembers the loss of love that had occurred before the relationship finally ended. He cleverly links the two levels through weather imagery; it is the wind which is confusing and tormenting him as he writes, and so in remembering their happy days together he describes it as a time "when our day was fair".

Why this scores high marks

ANALYSIS: Your answer gives a detailed **analysis** of the poet's theme – even though you have been told the poem is about loss, you have seen that this **operates at two levels**.

LINKS: You have made excellent **links and comparisons** between different parts of the poem, and between the theme and how the language is used to convey it.

REFERENCES: You have said clearly **how rhythms and sounds contribute to the overall meaning** of the poem so that the quotations support your argument.

Don't forget ...

The purpose of answering questions about poetry is to show that you appreciate the writer's ideas and feelings and how these are conveyed to the reader, mostly through the language but also through other features such as rhythm and structure (rhyme, repetition, stanza patterns, etc).

You will need to identify and describe some of the techniques used by the poet and the effects they have on you, the reader.

There are no right or wrong answers in how you react to a poem. Your own personal response is most important, but so also is the ability to suggest alternative meanings.

You must be able to support what you say by using evidence from the text – this could be a general reference or, better still, an actual quotation.

It is vital that you explain precisely how language works in a poetry text – you need a technical vocabulary (metaphor, simile, onomatopoeia, etc) but you must explain, not merely identify, devices.

You must express yourself clearly and logically – the examiner cannot reward answers which are difficult to understand and which do not put together a coherent argument.

Key skill – selecting material

- When asked to **support your answer** you must select **appropriate details** from the text.

- It is a good idea to make actual marks on the text. **Underline or highlight** words, phrases or sentences which will fit your answer as you think about the question(s).

- Decide which details you will refer to in **general terms** (probably those which emphasise the main theme or idea in a text) and those which you will **quote directly** (where there is an interesting use of language which you will comment on).

- Choose **a few relevant quotations** and analyse their effectiveness, rather than filling up your answer with a huge number of references about which you say very little.

- Try to **build some quotations into your own sentences** so that they read smoothly (for example, *Hardy tells us that his wife wore an "air-blue gown" when he first met her …*).

- Where you need to **set quotations apart** from your own words, make it clear that you are using a quotation by leaving blank lines before and after it and by enclosing it within inverted commas.

What the examiners are looking for

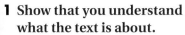
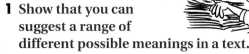

To achieve a Grade C, your response to reading poetry must:

1 Show that you understand what the text is about.

- You must find ways of explaining the obvious, 'surface' meaning and also show that you have some idea of what is 'between the lines'.

2 Show that you can make a personal response to the text.

- Explain what you feel about people and situations. Do you sympathise with them or not? Do you understand why people have particular ideas or attitudes?

3 Show that you can comment on aspects of the writer's style, and on the effects it achieves.

- Explain how the writer's choice of words helps you see certain meanings on or below the surface, perhaps through unusual or unexpected words, for example.

- Explain how the words or images make you feel about people and situations.

- Is there much description of feelings and ideas as well as of people, places and events? If so, does this allow you to understand the writer's point of view – and do you find it sympathetic or appealing?

4 Use details from the text effectively.

- You can refer to the text or quote directly from it – preferably the latter if you are referring to language.

- You must **use** your references and quotations, in other words by explaining what they show about the people or the theme, the ideas or the writer's use of language.

5 Present your answer clearly and logically.

- The examiner must be able to follow what you are saying.

- You should be putting forward a structured point of view (an argument), not just a collection of separate thoughts.

To achieve a Grade A, your response to reading poetry must:

1 Show that you can suggest a range of different possible meanings in a text.

- You should speculate and be prepared to be imaginative – but make sure that your suggestions are rooted in textual detail.

2 Analyse how successfully the writer's techniques convey meaning to you.

- You should be confident in making judgements, for example about how and why you do or do not like the way the writer has used certain images to describe a person or situation.

3 Relate details in the text to each other.

- You must show that you can take in the whole text, for example by comparing or contrasting ideas or uses of language at different places in the text.

4 Integrate references and quotations into your answer.

- You should try not always to set out quotations or references separately, but to make them sometimes flow into your writing by including them within sentences.

5 Develop and sustain your argument.

- You must develop the main points of your answer in considerable detail and link your ideas into a convincing and original overall approach.

- You must present a logical and coherent point of view, and not contradict yourself.

Typical exam question

Read *A View of Llandudno.*

Further along the front there stood a clutch of guesthouses and a few of them had vacancy signs perched in their windows. I selected a place that looked reasonable enough from the outside – it promised colour TV and coffee-making facilities, about all I require these days for a lively Saturday night – but from the moment I set foot in the door and drew in the mildewy smell of damp plaster and peeling wallpaper, I knew it was a bad choice. I was about to flee when the proprietor appeared and revealed that a single room with breakfast could be had for £19.50 – little short of a swindle. It was entirely out of the question that I would stay the night in such a dismal place at such an extortionate price, so I said, 'That sounds fine,' and signed in. Well, it's so hard to say no.

My room was everything I expected it to be – cold and cheerless, with ugly furniture, grubbily matted carpet and those mysterious ceiling stains that bring to mind a neglected corpse in the room above. Fingers of icy wind slipped through the single, ill-fitting window. The curtains had to be yanked violently before they would budge and came nowhere near meeting in the middle. There was a tray of coffee things but the cups were disgusting and the spoon was stuck to the tray. The bathroom, faintly illuminated by a distant light activated by a length of string, had curling floor tiles and years of accumulated muck packed into every corner and crevice. A bath was out of the question, so I threw some cold water on my face, dried it with a towel that had the texture of a Weetabix and gladly went out.

Bill Bryson

Bill Bryson clearly hates the guesthouse in Llandudno in which he stayed.
How does he convey his feelings to you?   [10 marks]

In your answer comment on:
● his use of fact and opinion;
● his choice of language;
● the way he creates mood and atmosphere.

What are the key words in this question?

● *Hates* is a very strong word which you will have to reflect through your choice of detail from the passage.

● *How does he convey his feelings* requires you to think about the techniques the writer uses, such as the **choice of language**, or the **mix of fact and opinion**, not just the content he includes.

● *Comment* means that it is not enough to list or refer to words or ideas. You have to say something about their contribution to the effect of the passage – that is, the way the writer **creates mood and atmosphere**.

Grade C answer

He shows his feelings through describing the awful smell and shabby conditions as well as the overpricing of the room. He gives a fact about what the room costs but his opinion is that it is too much. Everywhere is dirty and disgusting and he exaggerates this by comparing the towel to a Weetabix which is a rough kind of cereal. He makes it seem dark and gloomy when he describes the bathroom light and how difficult it is to turn it on.

Good points

CONTENT: Your answer does cover all three bullet points.

REFERENCES: You have referred to quite a number of details in the passage.

EXPLANATION: You have explained why one of the details is effective.

How to score higher marks

UNDERSTANDING: You could be more **precise in your choice of detail** so that the examiner realises that you have read the passage carefully.

REFERENCES: You could use direct **quotation**, especially when commenting on the writer's use of language.

STRUCTURE: You could make your answer more **structured**, and less a collection of separate points.

A better answer

An answer which included the points mentioned would read something like this:

Bill Bryson conveys his hatred of the guesthouse in a number of ways. First, he expresses a strong opinion about the price. He states the fact that it cost £19.50 for bed and breakfast, which some people might consider reasonable, but then he describes it as "little short of a swindle" and "extortionate": these words are usually associated with crime or criminals, and so Bryson makes it seem as though there is something almost sinister about the place. His choice of language to describe the bedroom develops this atmosphere through details such as the filthy cups and spoon stuck to the tray, which Bryson clearly feels would poison him if he attempted to use them, as would the "accumulated muck" in the bathroom. All in all, Bryson finds the guesthouse not merely unpleasant, but almost threatening, and he conveys this mood by adding to factual description — such as the window that did not fit properly and the tiled floor of the bathroom — with carefully-chosen adjectives such as "cheerless", "ugly" and "disgusting".

Typical exam question

Read carefully the following passage. It is taken from *Designer Genes*, a book about genetic engineering aimed at teenage readers.

The first attempt to transplant a human heart was made by Dr Christiaan Barnard in South Africa in 1967. Then, the patient died quickly, but today the same operation can extend a life by twenty years. All kinds of human organ transplants save thousands of lives every year. They're becoming more successful all the time, mainly because new drugs like cyclosporin are used to disarm the natural defence system of the human body and prevent it from rejecting transplanted organs.

Transplants save lives and money. A kidney transplant costs £10,000, and the patient needs £3000 worth of drugs every year to keep them alive. It currently costs £18,000 every year to treat the same patient if a dialysis machine is used to do the work of their kidney and remove lethal waste products from their blood.

So it's hardly surprising that demand for organ transplants has risen, and that there just aren't enough spare organs to go round. Now, in the US alone, around 100,000 human organs are needed every year for transplant patients. In Britain, over 3000 desperately ill patients are waiting for a new heart.

Phil Gates

Answer the following question:
(i) How does the writer use both facts and opinions to support the point he is making?
(ii) What is the writer's attitude towards transplant surgery, and how do you know this?

What are the key words in this question?

- You are asked not just to identify *facts and opinions* but to explain the *use* the writer makes of them.
- You have to say what you think the main *point* of the text is.
- You have to look for clues which reveal the writer's *attitude* to his subject.

Grade A answer

(i) The writer's main point in this article is that both lives and money can be saved by using transplant surgery rather than other methods to treat conditions such as heart failure or kidney disease. To support this point, he quotes facts such as the lower cost of kidney transplants compared with dialysis and the much-improved success rate of heart transplants since the first attempt in 1967. He makes a number of statements which are based on fact, but may contain an element of opinion, for example that heart transplants "<u>can</u> extend a life by twenty years" – in other words, this is not always the case. The numbers of patients waiting for surgery are also qualified by words such as "around" and "over". There are very few simple opinions in the text – only the opening of the second paragraph when the writer comments "it's hardly surprising ...": some people who are squeamish about transplants, or who have religious objections to them, might be quite surprised at the increasing demand for this kind of surgery.

(ii) The writer's attitude is that transplant surgery is a good development in medical science. This is obvious from the content of the text; although he acknowledges that the first heart transplant patient died, he goes on to say how much more successful the operation is now, and how many people are waiting for it. Although the article is based on fact and does not try to mislead the reader, it does contain generalised statements such as "All kinds of human organ transplants save thousands of lives every year". This both reveals the writer's enthusiasm for the method and makes the reader think it must be a good thing if so many lives are saved – but we do not know how long the patients survive, or what their quality of life is. The writer's use of numbers also suggests his enthusiasm – he tries to impress the reader with the large cost savings transplants can make, and with the large numbers of patients who want this kind of surgery.

Why this scores high marks

UNDERSTANDING: You have made clear in part (i) **what you think the writer's main point is**, and have tied all your comments about fact and opinion into this.

POINT OF VIEW: You have made the very good point that **defining fact and opinion is not always easy**, and have **quoted examples** to make your point.

REFERENCES: In the second part, you have again **made your starting point clear** and then have used many **references** to the text to support it.

EXPLANATION: You have explained the writer's **techniques** fully, so that it is obvious you have understood the text very well.

Don't forget ...

The purpose of answering questions about non-fiction texts is to show that you understand the writer's ideas and attitudes and how these are conveyed to the reader.

You will need to identify and describe some techniques used by the writer and the effects they have on you, the reader.

Your own personal response is important, but you must remember to stick to the content of the text and not to bring in your own knowledge of a subject or topic.

You must be able to support your comments by using evidence from the text – this could be a general reference or, better still, an actual quotation.

It is vital that you explain precisely how language works in a non-fiction text. You are less likely to need a technical vocabulary (metaphor, simile, onomatopoeia, etc) than when responding to fiction texts, but you must look out for the use of individual words or phrases which convey a strong point of view.

You must express yourself clearly and logically – the examiner cannot reward answers which are difficult to understand and which do not put together a coherent argument.

You may be asked to re-present a point of view or argument in your own words – take care that you do not change what the writer says, and be sure that you are picking up the main points, not less relevant material.

Key skill – distinguishing between fact and opinion

- Facts will usually be presented as a **simple statement**, without any descriptive language, for example "the house cost £35,000" or "the election was won by the national party". Be careful, though: sometimes writers present statements as facts when there might be considerable **disagreement**, for example "adding fluoride to drinking water benefits health" or "America was discovered by Christopher Columbus".

- Some words, such as *probably, undoubtedly, everybody*, clearly **signal that a writer is expressing an opinion** rather than relaying a fact, for example: "everybody knows that Manchester United is the best football team in England".

- Do not worry about having **difficulty in deciding whether some statements are fact or opinion**. If you are able to explain the difficulty by commenting on the writer's manipulation of content and language you will be rewarded, not penalised.

What the examiners are looking for

To achieve a Grade C, your response to reading non-fiction texts must:

1 Show that you understand what the text is about.

🎯 You must find ways of explaining the obvious (usually factual content) and also what is expressed more subtly, often as opinion.

2 Show that you can make a personal response to the text.

🎯 Explain what you feel about the writer's ideas and suggestions. Do you agree with them or not? Do you understand why a particular argument is put forward, or why certain details and illustrations are used?

3 Show that you can comment on aspects of the writer's style and techniques, and on the effects it achieves.

🎯 Explain how the writer's choice of words helps you understand meanings and attitudes on or below the surface, for example through humour or exaggeration.

🎯 Explain how the words make you feel about ideas and situations. Is there a mix of fact and opinion? If so, does the writer use this to give you different points of view, or to try and persuade you to agree with the text?

4 Use details from the text effectively.

🎯 You can refer to the text or quote directly from it – preferably the latter if you are trying to show how the writer uses particular techniques to influence the reader.

5 Present your answer clearly and logically.

🎯 The examiner must be able to follow what you are saying, and you must ensure that you answer the actual question, not the one you would like it to be!

🎯 You should put forward a structured point of view, not just a list of separate thoughts.

To achieve a Grade A, your response to reading non-fiction texts must:

1 Show that you can recognise a range of different viewpoints and implications in a text.

🎯 You should speculate and be prepared to be imaginative – but make sure that your suggestions are rooted in textual detail!

2 Analyse how successfully the writer's techniques convey meaning to you.

🎯 You should be confident in making judgements about the way in which the writer has chosen vocabulary or used references to have a particular effect on readers.

3 Relate details in the text to each other and to the writer's overall purpose.

🎯 You must show that you can take in the whole text, for example by linking different comments or statements – is the argument logical and coherent, or is the writer simply working on the reader's emotions?

4 Integrate references and quotations into your answer.

🎯 You should try not always to set out quotations or references separately, but to make them flow into your writing by including them within sentences.

5 Develop and sustain your answer to give an overview of the text.

🎯 You must develop the main points of your answer in considerable detail and link your ideas into a convincing overall approach.

🎯 Non-fiction writing sets out to convey information, ideas, instructions to you: your answer should make clear whether the purpose has been achieved, and in what ways this has been done.

Typical exam question

Read 'Simply To Die For' and then summarise the discomforts and risks that people have endured for the sake of fashion.

Use **your own words** as far as possible.

Write about 250 words in total.   [20 marks]

Simply to die for

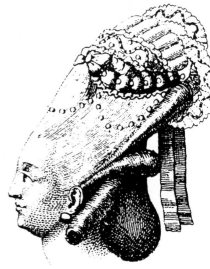

In the furore a few years ago that followed the banning of ankle-breaking Spice Girl-style platform trainers by the headmaster of a Somerset school, a Bristol-based orthopaedic specialist advised fans: "Put fashion second and your health first, because your legs have got to last you all your life, whereas a fashion fad will disappear in five minutes."

Unfortunately, despite their good intentions, both these men seem to have missed the point. You have to suffer for style, and long may it be thus. High fashion is often dangerous enough to carry a government health warning, and has been since the Middle Ages, when state and church issued edicts against the latest looks for reasons of moral safety.

Every fashion editor knows that only the brave and the bold can hope to cope with the latest sartorial developments. And every insider knows that Baby Spice's fatal error – Emma Bunton apparently tumbled off her platforms while filming in Turkey – was to forget that you're not *meant* to behave normally in high fashion, and never have been. In 16th-century Venice, for example, they had their own equivalent of the platform, called the chopine. Often worn 14 inches high, it required supports on either side. Moving at all in such footwear was extremely difficult.

The problem is that, since the garden of Eden, the human body has always been considered unfashionable. It is either too short, too thin or too fat, and so fashion tinkers with it accordingly.

An elongated head was considered the height of chic by ancient Egyptians and certain native American tribes. To get the right effect, babies had their heads tightly bound. Barbaric, perhaps, but this practice was still known in certain parts of provincial France as late as the middle of the last century. African tribes have stretched the ear lobes, elongated the neck and deformed the lower lip, all in the name

of fashion. And the West has not been far behind.

For centuries, nobody knew how to shape shoes to the foot. Straights, to be worn on either foot, were agony, and it was not until 1865 that shoes were designed for right and left feet. Even so, there was still the pain of stiletto heels to look forward to in the next century.

It is not just women who have suffered for fashion. Men have had to put up with their fair share of pain, too: the discomfort of the thickly wadded doublet favoured by the Elizabethans, made to hang over the stomach like a builder's beer belly; the inconvenience of the codpiece – all hot horsehair padding and difficulty of access: or the gloriously named galligaskins, heavy, wide, padded pantaloons. They make 1970's PVC trousers and leather pants – although sweaty and inclined to smell a bit like a horse after a brisk canter – seem a slight inconvenience.

Such nonsense did not stop with the Elizabethans. Think of 17th-century fops with their heavy wigs, tight corsets, thick make-up and red high heels teetering around royal palaces like an early Lily Savage. Or 19th-century cavalry officers in stays to narrow the waist and cork pads to give the calf a full and rounded shape. Or Russian courtiers whose breeches had to be so tight that they were put on wet. As they dried, they shrunk to a second skin, leaving nothing to the imagination. Lycra cycling shorts don't even come close. Little, of course, can compare with the heavily starched ruffs of the 17th century: moving the head required serious planning if the neck wasn't to be cut to ribbons.

In the 18th century the zinc-based make-up used to whiten the faces of both men and women left the rich and fashionable pock-marked and raddled by the time they were 30. It was a time when women wore their hair so elaborately high that they could only

travel in a coach if they knelt down. These hairstyles were so costly that the wearers left them untouched until lice and vermin were crawling through them: legend claims birds even nested there.

Perhaps the earliest fashions to die for – literally – were conceived in post-revolutionary France, where women wore thin calico dresses with little underneath. To mould them to the body, they were dampened with wet sponges. These fashionable ladies, know as *merveilleuses*, then stepped out in all weathers with their wet clothes clinging to them. Their penchant for this fashion extreme even led to a new illness, linen flu, which carried a fair few of them off prematurely.

Even keeping up with the latest style of Victorian dress – which set out to cover and conceal every inch of a woman's shape – could, at the very least, lead to illness and, occasionally, prove fatal. The vapours and other mysterious digestive problems that characterised Victorian femininity were caused by excessive tight lacing of corsets while crinolines regularly caused the death of fashionable young women. As they whisked past open fires, their skirts frequently caught alight, the flames fanned into a fury by the draught caused by the crinoline; worse still, nobody could get close enough to smother the blaze.

Similarly, in the 1920s, Oxford bags were so wide that men frequently tripped over themselves in them – just like hippies in their flares 50 years later. To try to cycle in them was the kiss of death. Even so, cyclists usually got off more lightly than dancer Isadora Duncan, whose fashionably flapping scarf caught in the wheel of her smart roadster and choked her to death in less then a minute.

So the discomforts and dangers we put up with today – from over-tight trousers to Hussein Chalayan's awkward mouth jewellery and Alexander McQueen's jackets sprouting precarious gazelle horns – are nothing compared to some of the killers from the past. And anyway, as the old trade saying goes: "Real fashion – agony, my pet, but always worth it."

What are the key words in this question?

- *Summarise* indicates that you should make a shortened account of the article, not bring in your own views.
- *Discomforts and risks* and *endured* show that you should maintain the writer's attitude towards the subject.
- *Use your own words as far as possible* means that you should not waste time trying to think of replacements for common or key words.
- The number of *words in total* should be followed as closely as possible.

Grade C answer

Headmasters and doctors tell people to be more sensible about what they wear but people like to be fashionable. Fashionable clothes have always been uncomfortable, e.g. shoes in Venice which were like modern platform soles made it hard for people to walk without falling over, just like Baby Spice. People have always wanted to change the way they look. Sometimes they make heads, or parts of heads like their lips and necks, different shapes in Egypt, Africa and America. This even went on in France with babies in the last century. Shoes for left and right feet were only introduced in the middle of the nineteenth century. Men as well as women have had to suffer, e.g. leather pants. Men wore make-up and high heels and padding, or sometimes very tight clothes and ruffs which could cut their necks to pieces. Women's hair was sometimes so tall they had to bend down in coaches and it became very dirty as well, but they didn't clean it because their hairstyles were so expensive. Clothes were sometimes dangerous if they

Good points

LANGUAGE: You have used your own words, e.g. *suffer* instead of *put up with*, *hard* instead of *difficult*.

STRUCTURE: You have worked systematically through the article.

WORD COUNT: You have kept within the word count (227 words used).

were too tight or wet or could catch on fire and were so big that no-one could get near enough to put the flames out. In modern times, people have fallen over their trousers or have been strangled by scarves. But fashion is worth it even if it hurts.

How to score higher marks

STRUCTURE: Try to **group similar ideas** together, such as those about footwear.

FOCUS: Don't try to include every detail in your answer. Keep to the main points and **just a few illustrations** if you have the space – and don't introduce examples with *e.g.*

LANGUAGE: **Don't work unnecessarily at using your own words.** For example, there is no need to replace 1865 with all the words *in the middle of the nineteenth century*.

UNDERSTANDING: Be careful about understanding the writer's **tone**. For example, the reference to ruffs which could cut the wearer's neck to ribbons is not serious.

A better answer

An answer which included the points mentioned would read something like this:

Those who condemn fashion for being unsafe or unhealthy – which has included governments and the church – miss the point that, through the ages, people have been prepared to put up with discomfort or danger to keep up with the latest fads.

Footwear illustrates the point. Platform soles are nothing new – the chopine of 16th century Venice made movement hazardous. The agony inflicted by wearing stiletto heels is not new, as shoes made to fit left and right feet were unknown until 1865. Fashionable clothing has veered between extremes. It has involved padding stomachs and calves, while at other times, waists have been so pulled in by stays or tight lacing that fainting or illness has resulted. Illness has also been caused by wearing wet, clinging clothes, and even deaths have come about when Victorian crinoline skirts caught fire or when Isadora Duncan was strangled by her long scarf catching in a car wheel.

Nor has it just been clothing which sets fashion: some cultures have even altered the natural shape of the body itself by binding babies' heads to make them longer or by artificially extending ear lobes, lips and necks. Make-up was worn by men about town in the 17th century and later, women's complexions were damaged irretrievably by using zinc-based preparations to make them fashionably pale.

Nothing is really new in the world of fashion, and it seems that people are always prepared to put up with the downside in order to be fashionable.

Typical exam question

Look at the National Lottery advertisement.

This advertisement is trying to persuade us that the National Lottery is a good thing and that Camelot is the best company to run it. How does it try to do this?   [10 marks]

In your answer comment on:

- the headline;
- the layout;
- the use of facts and figures;
- the choice of words.

What are the key words in this question?

● All points that you make must focus on *how* the advertisement tries to *persuade* the reader.

● Notice the two issues that you need to bear in mind: the *Lottery* itself, and *Camelot* as the company which runs it.

● The bullet points give you a *structure* for your answer: *headline*, *layout*, the *use of facts and figures* and the *choice of words*.

Everyone in the UK should be delighted to see this week's National Lottery numbers.

In only its first year, The National Lottery has raised a total of twelve hundred million pounds for the Good Causes.

An amount that no other lottery in the world has ever raised in such a short period of time. And one that shows that the choice to appoint Camelot to run The National Lottery was indeed the right one.

The National Lottery is now a national institution, with over two thirds of the UK playing regularly every week.

Not only have the Good Causes benefited from its success, the Treasury has also received £530 million, £225 million has gone to retailers and over £2,000 million has been awarded in prize money.

(Our unaudited results for the 24 weeks to 16th Sept 1995 are Sales: £2,510.1 million. Prize winners: £1,271.4 million. Good Causes: £678.8 million. Lottery duty, tax and VAT paid to the Government: £325.3 million. Retailers: £128.3 million. Camelot profit after tax: £23.6 million.)

All figures that we think put what we make (less than a penny in the pound) into proper perspective.

We, of course, are delighted by how much has been raised for the Good Causes. And everyone else should be too.

Because without your help, as they say, none of this would have been possible.

November 10 95

PAY **Good Causes.**

SUM **Twelve Hundred Million** **£1,200,000,000**

Pounds Only.

P. O—

THE NATIONAL LOTTERY

CAMELOT
Operators of The National Lottery

The advertisement aims to attract the attention of "Everyone", that is, not only those who play the lottery in the hope of winning. It does this by emphasising the amount of money that it has raised for "Good Causes" rather than prize money. Through this approach, it aims to persuade the reader that the Lottery itself is therefore a good thing and that Camelot was clearly a good choice of company to run it.

The headline is extremely large in relation to the rest of the text and it has the most important word first. The font is a traditional one, and there is a simple contrast between the background and the lettering so that the words stand out without any distractions to the eye. From the headline, the reader's eye is carried naturally to the picture of the cheque, with the prominent words "Good Causes" which answer the question "Why?" which may have formed in the reader's mind.

Facts and figures are used to support the claims that the Lottery is good, and that Camelot runs it well. The figures quote such large amounts of money that almost everyone is bound to be impressed by them. These are backed up by facts (or what we have to assume are facts) such as "no other lottery in the world has ever raised [this amount] in such a short time". So many figures are quoted that the reader is likely to just accept them.

Finally, the language is used to keep the reader involved – the advertisement uses "we" and "you" to make it sound as though some friendly people (rather than a vast, impersonal company) are speaking directly to the reader. The use of upper case letters for the words "Good Causes" whenever they are used reinforces the seriousness with which Camelot apparently takes its responsibilities, and it slips in a sort-of-apology for its profits, pointing out that they are really a tiny proportion of the money raised.

Overall, this is a simple, but carefully planned and effective, advertisement which will leave most readers believing that the National Lottery is a good thing and that Camelot is the best company to be running it.

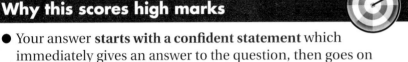

Why this scores high marks

- Your answer **starts with a confident statement** which immediately gives an answer to the question, then goes on to explain it in detail.
- You quickly sum up how the advertisement's approach **relates to the two issues** in the question.
- You then make a number of **sharp, detailed points** which respond to the **specific bullet points**.
- You show your **awareness of facts and opinions**, and how it may be difficult to distinguish between them.
- You give a **crisp conclusion** which neatly sums up the impact of the advertisement and your response to the overall question.

Don't forget ...

The purpose of answering questions about media texts is to show that you understand the writer's purposes and attitudes and how these are conveyed to the reader.

You will need to identify and describe some techniques used by the writer and the effects they have on you, the reader.

Your own personal response is important, because media texts are designed to make a personal impact on readers. Trust your reactions and explain what causes them.

You must be able to support your comments by using evidence from the text – this could, for example, be a general reference to layout features, or an actual quotation if you are responding to language.

It is vital that you explain precisely how language works in a media text. You are likely to come across words or phrases which convey a strong point of view, and sometimes devices such as humour (for example puns) will be used.

You must express yourself clearly and logically – the examiner cannot reward answers which are difficult to understand and which do not put together a coherent argument.

As in non-fiction texts, the mixture of fact and opinion is likely to be a key issue – make sure that you look for examples of how the text manipulates these.

Key skill – evaluating the presentation of texts

- If a question asks about presentation but does not define the word for you, think about:
  - the **appearance of the words** (font style and size, use of bold, italic or underlining, and maybe colour)
  - **layout** (headlines, subheadings, columns, bullet points)
  - **use of illustrations** (including graphs, charts, maps, etc.)
  - **use of the page** (positioning and size of the text relative to the whole page, landscape or portrait format, borders).

- It is never enough merely to **describe** these features. If you want to gain a Grade C or above, you must **evaluate** them – that is, explain what **effect** they have on the reader, and how or why this is so.

- In order to do this well, you need to **know and use the appropriate terminology** (see the first point above).

What the examiners are looking for

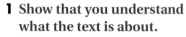

To achieve a Grade C, your response to reading media texts must:

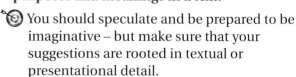

1 Show that you understand what the text is about.

◎ You must find ways of explaining the obvious purpose of the text and also what is 'between the lines' in an attempt to affect the reader's response.

2 Show that you can make a personal response to the text.

◎ Explain what you feel about the content and techniques used. Do you find them effective or not? Do you understand why the writer has adopted the chosen approach?

3 Show that you can comment on aspects of the writer's style and techniques, and on the effects they achieve.

◎ Explain how the writer's choice of language serves the purpose of the text, maybe through using unexpected humour or shock tactics, for example.

◎ How do presentational techniques help to convey the desired message?

4 Use details from the text effectively.

◎ You should both refer to general features of the text and quote directly from it.

◎ You must **use** your references and quotations, in other words **explain** what they show about the writer's purpose and the text's effect.

5 Present your answer clearly and logically.

◎ The examiner must be able to follow what you are saying.

◎ You should be putting forward a structured point of view, not just a collection of separate thoughts.

To achieve a Grade A, your response to reading media texts must:

1 Show that you can suggest a range of different possible purposes and meanings in a text.

◎ You should speculate and be prepared to be imaginative – but make sure that your suggestions are rooted in textual or presentational detail.

2 Analyse how successfully the writer's techniques convey meaning to you.

◎ You should be confident in making judgements about the effect the text has on you, and why this is so.

3 Relate details in the text to each other.

◎ You must show that you can take in the whole text, for example by showing how words and pictures support each other and contribute to the overall meaning of the text.

4 Integrate references and quotations into your answer.

◎ You should try not always to set out quotations or references separately, but to make them flow into your writing by including them within sentences.

5 Develop and sustain your answer.

◎ You must develop the main points of your answer in considerable detail and link your ideas into a convincing overall approach which makes a clear judgement about the effectiveness of the text.

Text A and Text B are newspaper articles about the Government's plans to introduce compulsory homework.

Compare how the story is presented in these two articles.

In your answer, you should comment on:
- the views expressed
- use of language
- layout and presentation.

[20 marks]

TEXT A

IT'S WRONG TO GIVE THE UNDER 12s HOMEWORK

Experts rap Blunkett plan

by Richard Garner, Education Correspondent

PLANS to set compulsory homework for primary schoolchildren are condemned in a report by education experts out today.

As the Government calls for 20 minutes study a night for five-year-olds and 50 minutes for 11-year olds, the report says: "Homework is not always a good thing."

Researchers Dr Susan Hall and Dr Richard Cowan warn there is not evidence it will improve standards and every chance it will fuel rows with parents.

Their verdict comes in the wake of detailed Government guidelines on extra study at home – and as a network of after-school clubs is set up across the country.

The report says while homework is valuable at secondary level, the case at primary is "less clear".

As long ago as 1935 school inspectors urged a ban on homework for under-12s because it made them too tired for lessons at school.

Dr Cowan told The Mirror: "Too much work can cause mental fatigue for youngsters.

Games

"Also there are worries that those from poorer homes don't have the conditions to do homework."

Instead of locking children away, they could "learn from just playing games with each other, or from adult company."

Homework can create "extreme tension" in families as parents try to help out. Mums and dads should cope with English but might find maths for older pupils difficult.

ADVICE: Blunkett

What the Government wants

FOUR and five-year-olds – 20 minutes: 10 minutes reading with parents, 10 minutes reading alone and doing sums with parents.

Sixes and sevens – 30 minutes: 20 reading with parents and 10 reading alone and practising sums.

Eights and nines – 40 minutes: half reading with parents, half homework.

Tens and 11s – 50 minutes: 20 reading and 30 homework.

At secondary level, 14-year-olds should do up to two hours a night.

The report for the British Psychological Society also says teachers can find homework too time-consuming to set. It can be poorly thought out.

Education Secretary David Blunkett's guidelines suggest 10 minutes reading with parents for the fours and fives and 10 minutes reading alone and doing sums.

Time goes up to 50 minutes at 10 and 11, including 20 minutes reading.

A spokesman for Mr Blunkett defended his advice, saying it was based on the "experience of successful schools".

The Mirror, Friday 18 September 1998

Blunkett sets targets for daily homework

David Charter on how ideas from the private sector are catching hold

MINISTERS want four-year-olds to do 20 minutes of homework a day as part of the crusade to raise standards in the three Rs.

David Blunkett, the Education Secretary, laid down homework guidelines for all ages yesterday, saying state schools should learn from the time children spent "cramming" in independent schools.

Mr Blunkett said a network of after-school clubs being created by the Government would give all children the advantages of those in the independent sector. The clubs would mirror the boarding school system of prep, or supervised homework.

Recent research showed that almost half of children in the top year of state primary school received no homework. Mr Blunkett announced that £200 million of lottery money would be used to fund nearly 10,000 after-school study clubs to give teachers no excuse for not setting every ten-year-old 50 minutes' homework a day.

"If it makes a difference for the children of parents who buy education, there is no reason why it should not make the same difference for those who cannot afford to," he said.

The Education Secretary said he was keen to learn from independent schools, which also provided more work for children during their holidays. "If something is working well, we will plagiarise it." The summer literacy and numeracy schools were a state version of private "crammers", he added.

The homework guidelines announced yesterday would help schools to draw up their home/school contracts with parents, Mr Blunkett said. He also praised the development of telephone hotlines set up by schools so that parents could find out what their children had been set for homework. He added: "Many parents are unsure, particularly at primary level, whether children should normally expect to be set homework at all. We have no power or intention to dictate in detail to parents what they do. What we can do is to indicate to people what is working and ask them to take on the responsibility that is rightly theirs."

The guidelines would give teachers and parents "sensible and realistic benchmarks on the amount of homework different age groups at primary and secondary schools might be expected to do".

He emphasised that, particularly for the youngest children, the Government was not suggesting formal homework. For four and five-year-olds, activities might largely consist of parents reading with their children and helping them to count for 20 minutes a night.

The Incorporated Association of Prep Schools praised the Government's intentions but said that homework was more about quality then quantity.

Nigel de Gruchy, general secretary of the National Association of Schoolmasters and Union of Women Teachers, said: "Homework is an important part of the learning process. Every child should have some at some time. But how much and when must be a matter of professional judgment."

Mr Blunkett said he did not want to spread misery among the nation's children. "All across the country, I can envisage little lads sitting on walls, swinging their feet, saying as I walk by: 'You're a miserable so and so, Mr Blunkett. More homework and fewer chips.'

"But I'm not a miserable so-and-so. We are in favour of homework, but we are in favour of homework that is rewarding, enjoyable and fun."

20 MINUTES FOR FOUR-YEAR OLDS	
PRIMARY SCHOOL	
Age	**Time**
4	20 minutes (includes 10 minutes' reading)
5 and 6	30 minutes (includes 10 minutes' reading)
7 and 8	40 minutes (includes 20 minutes' reading)
9 and 10	50 minutes (includes 20 minutes' reading)
SECONDARY SCHOOL	
11 and 12	45–90 minutes
13	60–120 minutes
14 and 15	90–150 minutes

The Times, Wednesday 22 April 1998

What are the key words in this question?

- *Compare* means that you must make sure you write a substantial amount about both articles, drawing attention to **similarities and differences** in them.
- *Comment* reminds you to explain the **effectiveness** of features you describe.
- Mention of the writers' *views* indicates that you should try to identify what each thinks about the Government's proposal, and especially **how this is conveyed to you** through the choice of *language*.
- *Layout and presentation* are crucial aspects of non-fiction and media texts, and you will need to consider how they **contribute to the impact** of each text.

Grade C answer

Both texts start out by mentioning the Government's plans for homework for young children, but they have different headlines which will have made readers come to the start of each article with different impressions of what the writers feel about the plans. The headline to Text A clearly shows that the writer does not agree with the homework plans, while the headline from Text B does not convey such an obvious view. The writer seems more likely to agree with the plan, but it is quite a neutral form of words. The Mirror text then only expresses a view about Mr Blunkett's plans in the last three paragraphs, but the Times article is giving the writer's views about the homework plans all the way through. The language in Text A is more simple than that in Text B. Text A mentions "mums and dads", but Text B talks about "parents". This is because Text A comes from a tabloid newspaper (the Mirror) and Text B from a broadsheet paper (the Times). Broadsheet readers want more detailed articles with more difficult language than tabloid readers.

The layout of the two texts is quite different. The headline to Text A is in bold capitals and Text B only has a capital letter for the first word so it does not stand out as much. Words like "wrong" and "rap" in the headline and subheadline to Text A put

Good points

STRUCTURE: You have followed the structure of the task well, so your answer covers all the general aspects required.

INTRODUCTION: You make a good start by referring to the expectations set up by the headlines and how these are followed up in the main text.

MEDIA KNOWLEDGE: You show some knowledge of the difference between tabloid and broadsheet newspapers.

over the writer's dislike of the homework plan but there are no words like these in the headlines to Text B. Text A has a picture but Text B has a chart, which again is because of tabloid and broadsheet differences.

How to score higher marks

REFERENCES: You could make **more specific reference to details**, for example the differences in the language used by the two writers – the sentence and paragraph structures as well as individual words.

DEPTH: You should not **over-simplify comparisons** between tabloid and broadsheet newspapers.

EXPLANATION: You need to **remember to explain effects** all the way through your answer: it starts well, but ends up just describing rather than explaining.

Grade A answer

An answer which included the points mentioned would read something like this:

The views expressed in these articles are quite different, and we realise this straightaway from the headlines; while The Times is quite neutral towards Mr Blunkett's proposals, The Mirror makes them sound unacceptable ("it's wrong") and silly (as they have been "rap[ped]" by "experts"). The fact that the headline in The Mirror is in bold capitals seems to make it scream out from the page, while the headline in The Times is altogether more reserved, both in language and printface.

The difference in the views expressed continues through the main text. Text A is mostly about the experts who disagree with the homework proposal, while in Text B there is a full explanation of the proposal together with information about why it has been made. Only the last three brief paragraphs of Text A, together with a box beneath the headline, actually detail what it is that the writer is objecting to.

The language in Text A is mostly straightforward ("mums and dads"), and each paragraph consists of just one sentence, although some of these sentences are quite long. However, there is some clever use of language such as the words "condemned" and "verdict", which set up an image of the homework proposals being put on trial. Many paragraphs in Text B contain more than one sentence, and there is a lot of variation in the language used, for example from "You're a miserable so-and-so" to references to "prep" and "crammers", which are perhaps closer to the experience of the typical Times reader than the typical Mirror reader.

The two layouts are again very different. The main part of Text A is in a single column, while Text B is laid out as a symmetrical block so that attention is drawn to the whole text rather than just to the headline. There is no picture in Text B, which seems to reinforce its neutrality, but Text A places a picture of Mr Blunkett very prominently under the headline so that readers can identify this unpopular proposal with an actual person. Although Text B appears neutral on the surface, its constant references to fee-paying schools may hint that it is working on possible snobbery in its readers to make them think that the proposals must be good if they are borrowing ideas from private education.

Why this scores high marks

REFERENCES: All your comments are backed up by **reference to the texts**.

UNDERSTANDING: You take an **overview** of the articles as well as mentioning precise details.

AWARENESS OF LANGUAGE: You are aware that the **tabloid** article may come across as easy to read but that it is **skilfully written**.

AWARENESS OF BIAS: You show **high-order reading skills** in recognising that there is a potential bias in Text B as well as in Text A – it is clever to end your answer by **raising a speculative suggestion about the broadsheet**.

Don't forget ...

The purpose of comparing non-fiction and media texts is to show that you understand the writers' different purposes and attitudes and how these are conveyed to readers.

You will need to identify and compare some techniques used by the writers and the effects they have on you, noting similarities and differences.

Your own personal response is important because non-fiction and media texts are usually designed to make a personal impact on particular readers, so trust your reactions and explain what causes them in the content, style or presentation of the texts.

You must be able to support your comments by using and comparing evidence from the texts. This could, for example, be a general reference to layout features or an actual quotation if you are responding to language.

It is vital that you explain precisely how language works in the texts – you are likely to come across words or phrases which convey a strong point of view and sometimes devices such as humour (for example puns) will be used.

In many texts, the mixture of fact and opinion is likely to be a key issue – make sure that you look for examples of how the texts manipulate these.

You must express yourself clearly and logically – the examiner cannot reward answers which are difficult to understand and which do not put together a coherent argument.

Key skill – making cross references

- Establish the **purpose and audience** of each text: this will give you a **focus** for the comments you make about them, including comparisons and contrasts.

- To gain high marks, introduce a general point – for example the use of illustrations – and then **compare** how **both texts** approach this: don't go through all the features of one text and then through all the same features of the other text separately.

- Make sure that you **comment on precise details**, for example about style of language or range of content, rather than making vague generalisations.

- Be prepared to say **which text is more successful** – but remember that this judgement should be made in terms of who the text is for, and what it is setting out to do, rather than which of them you enjoyed more.

What the examiners are looking for

To achieve a Grade C, your response to comparing non-fiction and media texts must:

1 Show that you understand what both texts are about and what the purpose and audience of both texts is.

- You must find ways of explaining the obvious 'surface' meaning and also what is 'between the lines'.

- You must show that you know whether texts are aimed at teenagers or adults, for example, or a particular group of people, and whether they are giving information or trying to be persuasive.

2 Show that you can make a personal response to both texts.

- Do you understand why the writers are communicating particular ideas or attitudes?

- Which do you find more convincing in relation to the target audience for both texts?

3 Show that you can comment on aspects of the writers' styles, and on the effects they achieve.

- Explain how the writers' choice of words helps you understand meanings and implications.

- How do presentational techniques help to convey the desired message?

4 Use details from the text effectively.

- You can refer to the text or quote directly from it – preferably the latter.

- You must **use** your references and quotations, in other words **explain** what they show about the writers' purposes and the effects achieved by the texts.

5 Present your answer clearly and logically.

- Present a structured point of view which continually compares the texts, not just a collection of separate thoughts about each of them.

- If required, make clear your preference for one text rather than the other, together with a summary of the reasons why.

To achieve a Grade A, your response to comparing non-fiction media texts must:

1 Show that you can suggest a range of different possible meanings in the texts in relation to their target audiences and purposes.

- You should speculate and be prepared to be imaginative – but make sure that your suggestions are rooted in textual or presentational detail.

2 Analyse how successfully the writers' techniques convey meaning to you.

- You should be confident in making judgements about the effect the texts have on you, and why this is so, and about their comparative success in terms of audience and purpose.

3 Relate details in the texts to each other.

- You must show that you can take in the whole of both texts, for example by comparing content or language in different parts of them, or how aspects of different presentational techniques affect overall meaning.

4 Integrate references and quotations into your answer.

- You should try not always to set out quotations or references separately, but also to make them flow into your writing by including them within sentences.

5 Develop and sustain your answer.

- You must develop the main points of your answer in considerable detail and link your ideas into a convincing overall approach which makes a clear and consistent judgement about the effectiveness of the two texts, both individually and in relation to each other.

Typical exam question

This task will be marked for writing.
Spend about 40 minutes on this task.

Leave enough time to read through and correct what you have written.

Write a story entitled 'The End of a Friendship'.   [20 marks]

What are the key words in this question?

- *Leave enough time to read through and correct what you have written* – **accuracy** in spelling, punctuation and grammar is important.

- *Write a story* – write a **narrative account** in which something happens.

- The *title* itself – your writing must be **relevant**, not just a re-working of something else you once wrote which vaguely fits the bill.

Extracts from a Grade C answer

The beginning

Luke and Emma had been friends for a long time. They had first met when they went to secondary school. They were in the same class for most of their lessons and liked the same things. When they were older, they helped each other with their homework and then they started going out to the youth club together. Their other friends thought they were an item, but Luke and Emma did not really see it that way. They felt more like a brother and sister and so when a new girl, Becky, joined the school in Year 10 neither of them thought that it could possibly lead to any trouble.

Good points

INTRODUCTION: You set the scene clearly, and introduce a potential source of conflict.

SENTENCE STRUCTURES: There is some variety in the way you construct your sentences.

ACCURACY: Your spelling, punctuation and grammar is accurate, for example the spelling of **friends** and **secondary** and the placing of commas around **Becky**.

How to score higher marks

STYLE: Choose some **more interesting or precise words or phrases**. For example, instead of **liked the same things**, you could have written **soon realised that they had many interests in common**.

LANGUAGE: Avoid **slang** phrases like **an item** except in speech.

INVOLVEMENT: Use **dialogue and description** as well as plain storytelling to catch the readers' attention. For example, you could have started **"Hi, Luke," called Emma as they met at the corner of Manor Lane.**

Extract from the middle

Emma did not really believe her friends when they said Luke was two-timing her with Becky. Their friendship wasn't like that anyway. She did sometimes feel funny when she saw them talking and laughing together but she didn't take any notice of it. They still walked to school together but at the youth club Luke spent most of his time with Becky and soon they were going there together.

Good points

STRUCTURE: You have continued to tell a straightforward story which holds together well and is obviously building towards some kind of climax.

ACCURACY: Your technical accuracy is still good, for example the spellings of **believe** and **laughing**, and the correctly-placed apostrophes in **wasn't** and **didn't**.

How to score higher marks

STYLE: **Vary your style**, for example by changing the viewpoint to Emma's. The second and third sentences could be: *"I'm not that sort of friend to him," thought Emma. "Or am I? I don't understand the strange feeling I get when I see them talking and laughing together."*

LANGUAGE: Watch your **use of pronouns**: *they*, *them* and *their* sometimes refer to Luke and Emma, and sometimes to Luke and Becky – potentially confusing! The previous suggestion helps, but the last sentence really needs to begin with *Emma and Luke* rather than *They*.

The ending

Luke had never wanted it to end like that. He still wanted to be friends with Emma. Maybe more than friends. He didn't really understand what had happened except that he knew Becky was selfish and mean in a way that Emma never had been. His other so-called friends had let him down — he would never have fallen out with Emma if he had not let them get to him.

Good points

STRUCTURE: You bring the story to a definite ending with an overview of what has happened and what one of the main characters feels about it.

STYLE: The short sentences you use at the start of the paragraph are an effective contrast with the two longer sentences which complete the story.

ACCURACY: Technical accuracy is still high. The use of the dash shows your ability to use a range of punctuation.

How to score higher marks

STYLE: You could again make this more dramatic by **changing the viewpoint** from the storyteller to Luke, for example: *"What has happened between me and Emma? Becky means nothing to me. She's selfish and mean …"*. This would also allow you to **show your control over punctuating speech**.

LINKS: It can be a **good ending technique** to refer to the title. For example, you could have ended: *Was this worth the end of a friendship?*

This task will be marked for writing.

Spend about 40 minutes on this task.

Leave enough time to read through and correct what you have written.

Write a story about a memorable journey. [20 marks]

What are the key words in this question?

- *Leave time to read through and correct what you have written* – **accuracy** in spelling, punctuation and grammar is important.

- *Write a story* – in other words, write a **narrative account** about a journey, real or imagined.

- The title itself – the journey you describe must be *memorable*, so you will have to think of a setting, a character or an event which makes it so.

Extracts from a Grade A answer

The beginning

How were we to know what would happen that dreadful night? Could anyone have known? I think not. After all, it had been a normal day when we set out, a happy family then, to visit the house that was to become our new home in a few weeks' time.

Why this scores good marks

INVOLVEMENT: You have created a real **air of mystery** – the reader wants to know what has happened. Starting with questions which plunge the reader straight into the story is a powerful technique for gaining interest.

SENTENCE STRUCTURES: Your **use of contrast** between a simple, three-word sentence and the long, complex sentence which follows it is very effective in signalling the shift into an explanation of the situation.

STYLE: Your **use of repetition** in the structure and vocabulary of the first two sentences is another attention-grabbing device.

ACCURACY: **Technical accuracy** is faultless, including the use of an apostrophe in *weeks'*.

Extract from the middle

So here we were, marooned in the middle of the murky countryside which was unfamiliar to us all.

"Don't worry," said my father. "Worse things happen at sea."

"We're not at sea," said my delightful little brother in his delightfully bright and cheerful way.

"Might just as well be in all this rain, this bloo..."

"Language, dear!" chipped in my mother, concerned as ever about appearances and social niceties even though there was no other living soul within a radius of about two thousand miles.

Why this scores high marks

STYLE: You have successfully **created tension** through description, and **characterisation** through use of dialogue.

LANGUAGE: Your **choice and use of vocabulary** is excellent, for example the alliteration in the first sentence, and the repetition of *delightful – delightfully* which conveys the speaker's irritation with the little brother, and adds force to the otherwise ordinary word *little*.

STYLE: Your **use of humour and exaggeration** makes an effective contrast with the potential seriousness of the family's situation.

The end

So there we sat, huddled in the car as the waters rose round us, sloshing and slurping their way through the gaps beneath the doors.

"I can see a blue light," sang out my brother.

"Shut up, idiot!" I snapped at him. "We're not going to get out of here, not even with the help of little blue men from outer space."

"No, you be quiet!" commanded my father. "You're not helping much with comments like that."

As my mother was about to do her oh-dear-what-would-anyone-think-to-hear-us-arguing-like-that act it happened: a door was wrenched open and there was the most welcome, most handsome fireman I had ever seen.

"Welcome to Yorkshire," he said.

Why this scores high marks

STYLE: You have continued the engaging **mix of humour and tension** through contrasting the situation with the dialogue.

LANGUAGE: Your **use of language** is excellent – alliteration and onomatopoeia in the first sentence, characterisation of speakers through words such as *sang, snapped* and *commanded*.

PUNCTUATION: Your **use of punctuation** is faultless, not only in conventional ways but in the hyphenated phrase which describes the mother.

INVOLVEMENT: Your **sudden, tongue-in-cheek ending** satisfies readers but leaves them wishing there had been more!

Don't forget ...

The purpose of this kind of writing is to engage and sustain the interest of readers.

Narratives need not be highly original or complicated but need a convincing beginning and ending.

You should show that you can use a range of narrative devices, such as different viewpoints, different timescales (such as flashbacks) and a mix of description and dialogue.

Your language must be precise, imaginative and varied, so that you establish the mood or atmosphere that you want.

Your spelling, punctuation and grammar need to be as accurate as possible and need to show the range of what you can do.

Key skill – accurate spelling and punctuation

- Check your own work to **identify the most frequent spelling mistakes** and recognise any patterns in your mistakes, so that you can **learn rules** which will improve your accuracy.

- You must be able to spell **common words and less familiar words** which obey normal spelling rules; you will not be heavily penalised for getting the spellings of **irregular or unusual words** wrong, so don't play safe all the time in your choice of vocabulary!

- You must get **basic sentence punctuation** right, and also be able to punctuate speech properly. If you can use **more advanced punctuation**, such as colons, semi-colons and dashes, you will improve the variety in your writing.

What the examiners are looking for

To achieve a Grade C, your writing which sets out to explore, imagine or entertain must:

1 Show you are really involved in what you are writing about and who you are writing for.

- Narrative writing needs developed characters and settings (Who is it about? Where is it happening?) and a logical structure (Why is it happening?).

- Bear your audience in mind – what do they expect your writing to be about?

2 Gain and hold your reader's interest.

- You need to think of ways of beginning your story which will interest your readers.

- You need to plan your story so that they stay interested and want to read to the end.

- You need to plan and write an effective ending.

3 Use language which you have chosen carefully, and which is used for effect.

- Stories, descriptions and reflections need to involve readers, so you must use the best words and images you can think of – be imaginative, not careful!

- If you are writing dialogue, try to make characters sound different from each other.

4 Use a variety of sentence structures.

- Don't always use short, simple sentences. Try to include some longer, complex ones, especially to convey complex ideas or feelings.

- Contrasting sentence lengths is a good way of keeping your readers alert and of showing your control as a writer.

5 Use paragraphs and punctuation to make your meaning clear and logical.

- Readers must be able to follow and understand your story. Use paragraphs and other ways of structuring the text such as headings, blank lines, ellipsis (rows of dots), especially if you try anything complicated, such as flashback.

- Direct speech is useful in characterisation – but you must punctuate it correctly.

To achieve a Grade A, your writing which sets out to explore, imagine or entertain must:

1 Approach the question in an original but appropriate way.

- The content of your writing must relate to the question set, but your approach and style of writing can be different and unexpected.

- Unconventional openings and closures will be highly rewarded – as long as they work!

2 Use striking and original ideas.

- Your writing must not be entirely predictable – for example, you might use a modern version of a traditional story to convey a contemporary message.

3 Use sophisticated language to affect your reader.

- You need to show that you have a wide-ranging vocabulary which can express subtle ideas and establish an appropriate tone and feeling.

- Use devices such as alliteration or onomatopoeia and repetition.

4 Use a style of writing which is varied and challenging.

- Try to construct a story so that you can show the range and variety of language you can call on – for example by contrasting the speech of different characters with poetic descriptions using similes or metaphors.

5 Link ideas well by using connecting words, punctuation, paragraphs, etc.

- You need to show that you can write coherently and accurately, using as wide a range of punctuation as possible to express shades of meaning, and linking paragraphs with words which support the structure of your story (*then, after a while, when he had finished*, etc.).

- Think about using sophisticated structures as well – for example, telling a story from different viewpoints or using flashbacks in the narrative.

Typical exam question

Write a letter to a friend who has recently moved away from your area, **informing** him or her of recent events in your life and of plans for the next few months.

Your letter should be lively and interesting. [54 marks]

What are the key words in this question?

- *Informing* reminds you of the **purpose** of your writing – you have to tell the reader something!

- The audience is a *friend* and the form is a *letter* – so the style of writing you should aim for is **informal and chatty**. However, you must follow the **rules of letter-writing**, such as layout, starting with *Dear* and ending with *Love from*, for example.

- You are told to be *lively and interesting* – so although the purpose is to tell your friend about what's been going on since she or he left, it is also to **inform** her or him of **your reaction to these events** – so your letter needs to **include comments and opinions as well as facts.**

Extracts from a Grade C answer

The beginning

Dear Sarah,
Thanks for the letter you sent me. I wasn't sure if you were going to send one at first, but it finally came two months after you left. I'm sorry I couldn't write before but you didn't give me your address.

Good points

INVOLVEMENT: You have set the scene for your reader.

LANGUAGE: The language has the right amount of informality. You have used contractions (**wasn't**, **I'm**, **didn't**). You haven't made any mistakes with grammar or spelling – apostrophes are in the right place, and **address** is spelt correctly.

How to score higher marks

STRUCTURE: The writer's address, and the date, should be at the top of the letter.

ORIGINAL IDEAS: For example, the last sentence might have read: *I'm sorry I haven't written before, but you forgot one <u>tiny</u> detail – to give me your new address before you left!* This would give your writing a **more original and humorous twist**.

PUNCTUATION: The new sentence would allow you to show the **correct use of two pieces of punctuation** (dash and exclamation mark) and the use of underlining to emphasise a point.

The middle

Your letter goes on to tell Sarah about the new term at school, including details about teachers she did and didn't like, and about what some of your other friends have been doing. It includes tales about weekend jobs, boy- and girl-friends, etc. This is written in one long paragraph, most of which is similar to this extract:

> Robbie has been picked for the area team. Jenny isn't going out with him any more because he spends all his time training. Sam has given up her job at the hairdresser's but I think she's sorry now because she doesn't have much money to spend.

Good points

INVOLVEMENT: It holds the reader's interest – Sarah would want to know about these things.

How to score higher marks

CONTENT: You have forgotten the part of the question which asked for **future plans** to be included in the letter!

STYLE: The **sentence structure needs to be more varied**. For example, you could have written: *Although Sam is glad to have given up her job at the hairdresser's, I think she's sorry in some ways because she doesn't have as much money to spend.*

LINKING IDEAS: You have produced a long list of events. You would do better to **write more about fewer events**. You can then add details which really let your reader have a **clear picture of the important things** that have happened.

The ending

> So you see, lots has been happening since you left. Well, that's about all the news for now. Please write back soon — sorry again for not having been able to get in touch before. Miss you!

Good points

LINKS: The first three words (*so you see*) link back well to the start of the letter and give a satisfying feeling.

SENTENCE STRUCTURES: These are varied.

How to score higher marks

STRIKING IDEAS: You could have made a **stronger ending** by referring back to a detail which you know would arouse Sarah's interest, for example by writing: *Miss you – but not as much as Jenny's missing Robbie!!*

STRUCTURE: You need to **end the letter in the correct way** with, for example, *Love from* and your own name.

You have witnessed an accident.

Write an account to inform the police about what happened. [54 marks]

What are the key words in this question?

- *Inform* reminds you of the **purpose** of your writing – you have to tell the reader **precise information about something**.

- *Police* tells you the audience (reader) you are writing for.

- Together with the words *witnessed* and *account*, it suggests the **structure and tone** you should adopt: **formal and factual**.

Extracts from a Grade A answer

The beginning

It was Tuesday 5 July, at about 5 o'clock. The weather was dry, but overcast, and the roads were quite busy. As I turned into Newtown Avenue, I heard a vehicle approaching very quickly from behind me, and I remember thinking it could be hazardous as there were parked cars along both sides of the road which would restrict the driver's vision.

Why this scores high marks

APPROPRIATE: You realise that the police (the audience for the report) would want the report to give **factual details** such as time, place, weather conditions and so on, since the purpose of the account is to understand why the accident happened.

ORIGINAL IDEAS: You have included some **opinion** (*I remember thinking…*). This is only a passing comment; it does not interfere with the main point of the account, but it does make it **more interesting**.

LANGUAGE: You have **used language precisely** (…*dry, but overcast*,…). It is sometimes **sophisticated** (*hazardous* rather than the more predictable word *dangerous*).

STYLE: The third sentence shows you can write a **complex sentence which is interesting and readable**.

LINKS: You have used **good linking phrases**, such as *and I remember thinking* and *as there were*.

The middle – an outline plan

Your answer to this question needs to **follow a logical pattern**.

In informative writing, it is usually best to **tell things in the order in which they happened**, so as not to risk confusing readers.

Your accident report would need to **set out exactly what the witness saw, in chronological order**, with references to precise details like times, people's names, car registrations, etc.

Why this scores high marks

STRUCTURAL DEVICES: You would **use paragraphs to separate events**. You would **underline key references** such as names of people, times, vehicle registrations, etc. so that someone skimming the account for the most important facts would immediately see them.

The end

These are the facts as I remember them. I am quite clear in my mind that the cause of the accident was the speed at which the driver of the Sierra came down Newtown Avenue. As her vision was obscured, the driver of the stationary vehicle on King's Drive had no more than a remote chance of avoiding the collision. Please contact me at my home if you wish to clarify any details in this statement.

Why this scores high marks

LANGUAGE: You have used **sophisticated words and phrases** such as *obscured* and *no more than a remote chance*. You have **avoided potential spelling errors** in 'stationary' and 'collision'.
STYLE: You have used a **variety of sentence structures**. The language is consistently formal.
LINKS: You have moved neatly from the main, factual body of the account back to an expression of opinion which mirrors the beginning of your account.
APPROPRIATE: Your final sentence/paragraph **addresses the purpose and audience of the task directly**.

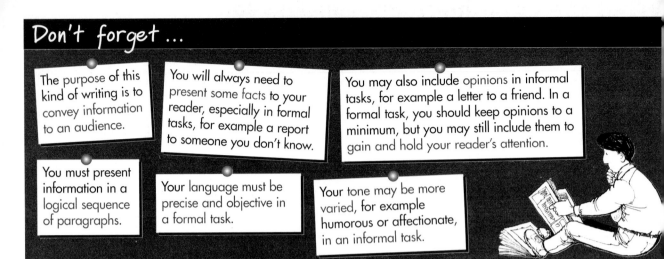

Don't forget ...

The purpose of this kind of writing is to convey information to an audience.

You will always need to present some facts to your reader, especially in formal tasks, for example a report to someone you don't know.

You may also include opinions in informal tasks, for example a letter to a friend. In a formal task, you should keep opinions to a minimum, but you may still include them to gain and hold your reader's attention.

You must present information in a logical sequence of paragraphs.

Your language must be precise and objective in a formal task.

Your tone may be more varied, for example humorous or affectionate, in an informal task.

Key skill – structuring your work

● Your **sentences** need to be **varied** to interest the reader and to show your grammatical skills. For example, here are three **simple** sentences:

– His car had broken down.
– He knew it was a serious problem.
– He went home by bus.

These could be made into a **compound** sentence by using **connecting words**:

– His car had broken down and he knew it was a serious problem so he went home by bus.

Alternatively, they could be made into a complex sentence which **makes the logical connection between the sentences clearer**:

– As he knew it was a serious problem when his car broke down, he went home by bus.

● You need to **use paragraphs** to help your readers follow your ideas:

– You need to **link sentences** within a paragraph by theme or topic.
– You need to **link paragraphs to each other** by logically sequencing what you are writing about.
– Make sure that your **opening paragraph sets out your purpose clearly**, and that your **closing paragraph brings the writing to a satisfying conclusion**.
– **Plan opening and closing paragraphs in detail**, even if you are working to a time limit: this will ensure that your work makes a good impression on the examiner when he or she starts and finishes reading it!

What the examiners are looking for

To achieve a Grade C, your writing which aims to inform, explain or describe must:

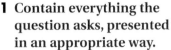

1 Show you are really involved in what you are writing about and who you are writing for.

- Informative writing always has a **purpose** (What is it giving information about?) and an **audience** (Who wants the information?).

- You need to sound as though you know your subject very well. You also need to get what you know across to your readers.

2 Gain and hold your readers' interest.

- You need to think of ways of beginning your writing which will really interest your readers.

- You then need to plan your writing so that they stay interested and want to read to the end.

3 Use language which you have chosen carefully, and which is used correctly.

- Information needs to be correct and precise, so you must use the most appropriate words you can think of. You need to spell them correctly, too.

4 Use a variety of sentence structures.

- Don't always use short, simple sentences. Try to include some longer ones – but don't write very complicated sentences just for the sake of it.

5 Use paragraphs and punctuation to make your meaning clear and logical.

- Information must be easy to follow and understand. You must break it into sections (paragraphs) to separate different ideas or topics.

- You must use full stops and capital letters correctly. You may need to use colons and semi-colons if you are listing things.

To achieve a Grade A, your writing which aims to inform, explain or describe must:

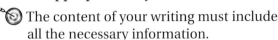

1 Contain everything the question asks, presented in an appropriate way.

- The content of your writing must include all the necessary information.

- Your style of writing must be exactly right for your audience (your readers).

2 Use striking and original ideas.

- Your approach must not be entirely predictable – for example, you might use humour to convey a serious message.

3 Use sophisticated language to get across your meaning.

- You need to show that you have a wide enough vocabulary to express subtle ideas and to establish a particular tone, for example light-hearted humour or seriousness.

4 Use a style of writing which is varied and challenging.

- You may sometimes choose to mix everyday language with more specialist terms, or to use rhetorical questions (*What is the point of this?*), for example.

5 Link ideas well by using connecting words, punctuation, paragraphs, etc.

- You need to show that you can use words such as *however, nevertheless, insofar as,* etc.

- You may need to use sub-headings, bullet points, underlinings or other presentational devices, as well as paragraphs.

Typical exam question

Your class has been invited to the local television studio to form part of the audience in a discussion programme. Write the set of **instructions** which your school might give out to the pupils going on the visit. You should include instructions on such things as:

- how to prepare for the trip
- what to wear
- when to meet and where
- how to behave
- what will be expected after the trip.

[54 marks]

What are the key words in this question?

- You are told to write a *set of instructions*, so you will be **advising** readers.
- *You should include* means that you **must cover the whole bullet-pointed list**.
- *How, what, when* and *where* all require slightly different types of advice.

Extracts from a Grade C answer

The beginning

You need to be well-prepared for the visit, so you should watch the news on television or read a newspaper in the week leading up to it. We will be discussing some people and events in the news as part of our English work as well, to help you understand and enjoy what is going on in the discussion at the television studio.

Good points

STRUCTURE: You have written a focused start, leading straight into the first bullet point about preparations for the visit.

IDEAS: You have added some sensible ideas of your own (i.e. that the discussion programme will be about current affairs) so that you can write detailed advice.

ACCURACY AND STYLE: Your writing is accurate and fairly easy to read, although the second sentence in particular is quite long and complicated to follow as an instruction.

How to score higher marks

PRESENTATION: Remember the task – this is a sheet that will be issued to pupils by the school, so it would almost certainly have a **heading** before plunging into the instructions. An underlined heading such as ***Visit to Newtown TV Studios by Year 11 on Friday 11 December*** would be helpful.

STYLE: When people are reading instructions or advice, they need to be able to see points quickly and easily. Think about using **bullet-pointed lists** to avoid long sentences, for example:

You will enjoy the discussion more if you:
- watch television news
- read newspapers
- join in discussions in English lessons

during the week before the visit.

The middle

On the day of the visit you should return to school at 5 o'clock so that we can all meet up to go to the TV studio together. You will need to bring a packed tea with you and if you want to stay behind after school that will be fine.

Good point

CLARITY: You have given a precise time for the meeting and have made it clear that pupils need to bring food with them.

How to score higher marks

PRECISION: Your instructions could be made **more precise** by telling the pupils exactly where to meet at school.

SENTENCE STRUCTURE: Your second sentence is a little **muddled**: it would be better to have the comment about staying at school linked with the meeting time rather than with the comment about a packed tea.

The ending

After the trip we will be back at school at about 10 o'clock and you should make arrangements for someone to meet you then. Remember that you are representing your school and we expect your very best behaviour. Anyone who lets the school down will be dealt with severely the next day.

Good points

CONTENT: You have given the important information that parents will want to know, about the arrival time back at school.

CONTENT: Instructions about behaviour would certainly need to be included somewhere on the sheet of instructions.

ACCURACY AND TONE: Your writing is accurate, and the tone sounds realistic, if rather negative!

How to score higher marks

EXTRA INFORMATION: You could have taken *what will be expected after the trip* in a **wider sense**, i.e. to include some instructions about keeping notes to use in follow-up activities in class.

TONE: You might have finished on a **more positive note**, for example by including a statement about how interesting an experience it will be and how it will help in the pupils' exam work.

> Write a speech for a classroom debate on a topic about which you feel strongly.
> You could choose a local, national or worldwide issue. [20 marks]

What are the key words in this question?

- *Speech* suggests a **formal response which must sound persuasive** when spoken out loud.

- You must choose a topic about which you feel **strongly** or you are unlikely to produce a convincing piece of work. Remember that this speech is for a debate.

Extracts from a Grade A answer

The beginning

I believe that there is too much testing of children in schools these days. Almost from the moment they enter nurseries or playgroups, small children who are little more than babies are subjected to tests which examine how they play together, how they speak and how much they can read or write. Surely that's what they go to school for – to learn these things? Why do they have to be so good at everything before they get there?

Why this scores high marks

CLARITY: You have **stated your topic firmly and confidently** right at the beginning.

SENTENCE STRUCTURES: You have used a **well-constructed longer sentence** which keeps listeners waiting for its subject (***little children***) and have used **repetition** of ***how*** to build up your exasperation effectively.

INVOLVEMENT: You have used two **rhetorical questions** to end the first part of your speech, so that listeners are drawn into your argument and are made to think about their own feelings.

Extract from the middle

You could say that there has always been testing in secondary schools, and that employers or universities need to know what school-leavers can do. Well, maybe that is so, but surely a few basic school examinations would be adequate for that purpose. After all, many companies use their own tests for employees in addition to the GCSEs or A Levels they already have. The government cannot have it both ways: either GCSEs are important and reliable, in which case they should be sufficient in themselves, or it is better for companies to set their own entrance tests, in which case why make pupils go through the trauma of taking GCSEs?

Why this scores high marks

EVIDENCE: You have continued to **use evidence well**, moving on from nursery schools to secondary schools.

APPROPRIATE: You have kept a **formal tone** (for example, not abbreviating phrases such as **there has** or **that is**) but the use of a word such as **Well** at the start of a sentence makes this sound like a **genuine speech**.

BALANCE: You have put forward a **coherent, balanced argument** in the last sentence.

LANGUAGE: In the last sentence, you have used the device of a **rhetorical question** to involve listeners in what you are saying, and have shown use of sophisticated vocabulary (**trauma**).

The end

In conclusion, I must say that I find the current attitude to testing children absurd. It causes anxiety among the children themselves and their parents. It relies too much on limited evidence of what they can do. It puts too much competitive pressure on teachers and schools. It is, in the end, pointless, as it only measures how good children are at tests, not how good they are at the skills they need in real life. Does a pig become heavier the more often you weigh it? I rest my case.

Why this scores high marks

STRUCTURE: You have presented it as an **obvious conclusion**, towards which your argument has naturally been leading.

SENTENCE STRUCTURE: You have used **repetition of sentence structure** (*It* + verb in present tense) to build up an engaging climax.

VOCABULARY: You have used more **good vocabulary** (*current attitude, absurd, anxiety, limited evidence, competitive pressure*).

STYLE: You have used **ironic humour** and a **firm closing statement** to end your speech in a strong, challenging manner.

Don't forget ...

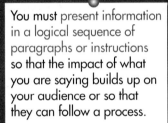

The purpose of this kind of writing is to persuade or assist an audience to believe something or to do something.

You will need to present some facts or evidence to your reader so that they understand why you are telling them certain things.

You should include opinions in many tasks, particularly argument or persuasion, but instruction or advice remain mostly factual.

You must present information in a logical sequence of paragraphs or instructions so that the impact of what you are saying builds up on your audience or so that they can follow a process.

Your language must be precise, especially for advice or instruction, but can be varied and engaging in argument or persuasion: you may need to work on the emotions of your audience by using humour or anger, for example.

Your tone and style must match the task – an emotive speech will need to sound very different from a set of instructions.

Key skill – connecting thoughts in writing

- Whatever kind of writing you are doing, your thoughts must be connected in ways which **help your readers follow your ideas and understand your attitudes**.

- **Sentences must be complete** in themselves, and must be linked carefully to each other, for example by using **conjunctions** such as *however, because, if*, etc.

- **Paragraphs need to follow logically** one from another. There are two ways of ensuring this:
  - have an overall plan for your work
  - use the right connectives between paragraphs in the same way that you use them between sentences (***It can therefore be seen that ...***, ***Nevertheless you might argue that ...***, etc.).

- In any piece of writing, know what your **main idea** is, and make sure that it recurs frequently – this helps your readers to stay with you, as well as helping you make your work **coherent and cohesive**.

- Make sure that every paragraph has a **topic sentence** which relates to an aspect of your overall main idea.

What the examiners are looking for

To achieve a Grade C, your writing which aims to argue, persuade or advise must:

1 Show that you have strong feelings about your subject-matter and an attitude towards your readers.

◎ Argumentative writing always has a **purpose** (Why is it presenting the case?) and an **audience** (Who do you want to persuade or advise?).

◎ You need to sound as though you know your subject very well, in addition to having strong feelings about it.

2 Gain and hold your readers' interest.

◎ You need to think of ways of beginning your writing which will really grab your readers' interest – perhaps by asking a rhetorical question or by making a challenging statement.

◎ You need to keep them interested by the impact of your writing and/or the evidence you use.

3 Use language which you have chosen carefully, and which is used powerfully.

◎ Information needs to be correct, but you can choose to present it in ways which suit your argument – for example by exaggeration, or dismissive humour.

4 Use a variety of sentence structures.

◎ In an argumentative piece, variations will keep your readers alert. Short sentences can be used to challenge or provoke, while longer sentences can be used to convey information.

5 Use paragraphs and punctuation to make your meaning clear and logical.

◎ Argument, persuasion or advice must be easy to follow and understand if it is to achieve its purpose. You must break your writing into paragraphs to clarify different ideas or aspects of the subject.

◎ You may need to use question marks and exclamation marks to emphasise important points. Use colons, semi-colons or bullet points if you are listing.

To achieve a Grade A, your writing which sets out to argue, persuade or advise must:

1 Contain sufficient information, presented in an appropriate way.

◎ The content of your writing must include the necessary information. Read the question carefully – you may be asked to present one point of view, or both sides of an issue.

◎ Be careful about only presenting one side of an argument – it can strengthen your case to acknowledge other views and then to point out why you disagree with them.

2 Use striking and original ideas.

◎ Your approach should not be entirely predictable – for example, you might use humour to convey a serious message about a controversial issue.

◎ Use anecdotes or references to news stories and so on to support your case – you do not have to rely entirely on your own knowledge and ideas.

3 Use sophisticated language to get across its meaning.

◎ You need to show that you have a wide-enough vocabulary to express subtle ideas and to establish a particular tone, for example light-hearted humour or total seriousness.

4 Use a style of writing which is varied and challenging.

◎ You may sometimes choose to mix everyday language with more formal language, or to use rhetorical questions (such as *What is the point of this?*), for example.

5 Link ideas well by using connecting words, punctuation, paragraphs, etc.

◎ Show that you can use words such as *however, nevertheless, insofar as*, etc.

◎ You may use sub-headings, bullet points, underlinings or other devices, as well as paragraphs, depending on the purpose and context for the writing.

Read again the two newspaper articles about homework in schools on pages 35–36 .

Based on comments made in the articles and on your own experience, analyse the benefits and disadvantages of homework for 10–11 year-olds. [20 marks]

What are the key words in this question?

- *Based on comments in the articles* – in other words, you need to introduce some of your **own ideas and experiences** as well.

- *Analyse the benefits and disadvantages* means something similar to 'compare', but requires you to go as fully as you can into all aspects of the issue, and to take a fairly dispassionate view of it – you are **not asked to argue a particular case** or to persuade readers to a particular point of view.

- Note the reference to a **specific age-group**.

Extracts from a Grade A answer

The beginning

Homework is an emotive subject for everyone involved: schools, parents and pupils. It can lead to arguments at home and at school, particularly if parents are dissatisfied with the work set, or the time their children spend on it, or if pupils do not have a suitable environment in which to do their homework and are blamed for this by their teachers. However, part of the government's agenda in raising school standards is to try to make the use of homework more consistent, and that is why the subject continues to receive considerable publicity. Recent newspaper articles have discussed David Blunkett's latest requirement for all schools to set homework across the age-range. In this essay, I shall consider the benefits and disadvantages of homework for 10–11 year-old pupils, that is, those in their final year of primary school.

Why this scores high marks

CONTENT: You have made a **strong opening statement** which is then **backed up by examples** of what this means.

LINKS: You have made a neat shift from this **general point** to a more **specific reference** to the current scene and to the sort of materials which are the stimulus for this essay.

EXPLANATION: You have made the **purpose of your essay very clear** by referring to the words of the task – but by explaining them, not merely repeating them.

VOCABULARY: You have used **sophisticated vocabulary** (*emotive, environment, agenda*).

LANGUAGE: This is **technically accurate**, for example the use of the colon in the first sentence, and the correct spelling of potentially difficult words such as *dissatisfied*. It also shows **control of a range of sentence structures**, for example the contrast between the short, direct opening sentence which states a point of view and the long, complex following sentence which analyses the idea in more detail.

Extract from the middle

The reaction of different people to these ideas is very interesting. On the one hand, David Blunkett feels that children in state schools should have the same advantages as those who attend private schools – in other words, an extension to the basic school day by the addition of a daily homework slot. On the other hand, researchers for the British Psychological Society have suggested that younger children may suffer mental fatigue, and they are aware (as are all my friends and myself!) that enormous tension can be caused at home by the conflicting demands of homework, television, friends, or other forms of pleasurable entertainment.

Why this scores high marks

ANALYSIS: Analysis should include considering a **range of views**: you have done this by reference to the newspaper articles and to your own experience, as required by the question.

BALANCE: You have not only included a balanced range of views, but have used **grammatical balancing** as well, i.e. by writing *On the one hand … On the other hand*.

LANGUAGE: Your **vocabulary is still wide-ranging** and you have introduced a welcome note of **humour**, correctly using brackets and an exclamation mark, which sustains the reader's interest.

In conclusion, then, I would argue that the benefits of homework for 10–11 year-olds probably outweigh the disadvantages. I believe that the skills required to live in our world include the ability to direct one's own work and to carry out research using the latest ICT facilities. Homework is a good way of giving some responsibility to children, especially those who are about to enter secondary school and will meet increasing demands for coursework and projects. Of course, it is necessary to keep this in balance, and there should continue to be a campaign to educate parents so that they are understanding and not too demanding. After all, homework should be an opportunity for parents and children to learn together and to share exciting experiences, not an occasion for arguments, threats and fallings-out!

Why this scores high marks

LINKS: You have brought your essay to a **firm conclusion**, which states the result of your analysis and **refers back to the wording of the question**.

SUMMARY: You have not repeated everything you have already written, but have stated three or four **new ideas which sum up your views**.

LANGUAGE: You have used **helpful grammatical constructions** which allow the reader to follow your argument, for example *In conclusion … , I believe that … , After all … .*

APPROPRIATE: You have continued to use **appropriately formal vocabulary**, but use a slightly less formal phrase (*fallings-out*) to end in a direct way which leaves your reader with the feeling that you have been a **persuasive but friendly** writer.

The purpose of this kind of writing is to assist your readers to understand your views about something.

You have to do this through a review of facts, evidence or opinions so that your readers understand why you are telling them certain things.

You then need to comment on this material, making clear the extent to which you agree or disagree with it.

You need to analyse the information in a logical sequence of paragraphs so that your readers can follow the process by which you have come to certain conclusions.

Your language should be formal and wide-ranging, but can be varied for particular effect, for example by the use of humour to make a point – which may involve using less formal or colloquial language.

Remember to use a wide range of grammatical constructions, correctly punctuated. Analytical writing should include some complex sentences, which offer opportunities for you to use colons and semi-colons, dashes, parentheses (brackets) and so on.

Key skill – writing for different purposes and audiences

● First, look for the **key word(s) in a writing task**, for example **describe**, **argue** or **analyse**. These words define your **purpose**, and tell you what **effect** your writing should have on your readers.

● Think then about the **kind of language** suggested by the key word(s):

– **describe** means you must carefully choose adjectives and verbs, for example, to give readers the clearest possible mental picture of what you are writing about

– **argue** means that you will be choosing emotive words or phrases (such as *Everybody knows that* …) to convey a strong point of view.

● Think about how to **structure your writing to meet its purpose**:

– a piece which is conveying ideas, either factually or argumentatively, needs to be logical and to build idea by idea

– a description or a narrative may be much looser, and can move to and fro from place to place, from person to person, or from one time to another.

● Whatever your purpose, think about the **audience**. If you were asked to write about how to use a word-processor, for example, you would do it very differently for an 8 year-old, or a teenager, or an elderly person who has no knowledge at all of ICT. This means that you will need to think about and adapt your:

– **content** (How much does your reader already know? How much information do you want or need to give?)

– **language** (What will your reader expect? What will be understood, for example technical terms or modern slang?)

– **style** (Formal or informal? Personal or impersonal? Layout and presentation?)

What the examiners are looking for

To achieve a Grade C, your writing which aims to analyse, review or comment must:

1 **Show you understand your subject matter and the needs of your readers.**

- Analyses/reviews always have a **purpose** and an **audience** (Who wants to know about these things, and why?).

- You need to sound as though you know your subject matter well. You also need to get an overview – that is, a review – of what you know across to your readers.

2 **Gain and hold your reader's interest.**

- You need to think of ways of presenting your comments which will interest your readers.

- You need to plan your approach so that they stay interested and want to read all your views.

3 **Use language which you have chosen carefully, and which is used correctly.**

- Review and analysis, especially if it is summing up information, needs to be correct and precise, so you must use the most appropriate words in your comments.

4 **Use a variety of sentence structures.**

- Try to keep your writing straightforward so that the points you are making come across clearly, but vary sentences where you can in order to keep readers interested. If you are analysing complex ideas, you will need to use some long and/or complex sentences.

5 **Use paragraphs and punctuation to make your meaning clear and logical.**

- Comments and conclusions must be easy to follow and understand. You must break your writing into paragraphs to separate different ideas or aspects of your analysis.

- You must use full stops and capital letters correctly. You may need to use question marks, or exclamation marks to emphasise important points. Use colons and semi-colons and maybe bullet points if you are listing ideas.

To achieve a Grade A, your writing which aims to analyse, review or comment must:

1 **Contain everything the question asks for, presented in an appropriate way.**

- The content of your writing must include all the necessary information, i.e. a full overview of the subject together with precise detail about significant aspects of it.

- Your style of writing and tone must be exactly right for your target audience and what it wants to know.

2 **Use striking and original ideas.**

- Your approach must not be entirely predictable – for example, you might use humour to convey a serious message, or quote selectively from a text in order to make a point. Adding relevant anecdotes about personal experiences can be effective.

3 **Use sophisticated language to get across its meaning.**

- You need to show that you have a wide enough vocabulary to express subtle ideas and to establish a particular tone, for example light-hearted humour or seriousness.

4 **Use a style of writing which is varied and challenging.**

- You may sometimes choose to mix everyday language with more specialist terms, or to use rhetorical questions or direct comments to the reader inside brackets, for example *You may feel that is not a very significant idea!*.

5 **Link ideas well by using connecting words, punctuation, paragraphs, etc.**

- You need to show that you can use words such as *however, nevertheless, insofar as*, etc.

- You may use sub-headings, bullet points and underlinings, or other presentational devices, as well as paragraphs, if this helps to organise your material.

Question 1

(In this passage, the story-teller, a fifteen-year-old boy called Matthew, is expressing his thoughts about his family and his school.)

There is a picture of me, in one of our photograph albums, when I was four years old. It shows a slightly goofy little kid standing outside the school gates with a great grin on his face. Underneath it is a label which says, "Matthew's first day at school."

"How come I'm smiling?" I asked my mum once.

"Because you were really excited about going to school," she told me.   5

"I was?"

"You certainly were. You loved it."

"What?"

"You used to run ahead of me every morning to get there."

Aren't little kids suckers?   10

School is just to keep you busy, that's all. I read once that in the Middle Ages, before school was invented, children used to run riot. So one day some wise-guy must have sat up and said, "Hey, I've just had a really good idea to get these kids off our hands. I think I'll call it school."

At eight o'clock on a Monday morning I used to think about that wise-guy and what I would like to do to him. This particular morning was no exception.   15

"Mum," I shouted downstairs, "where are the clean white shirts?"

"I don't know," she called back. "Try looking."

I once watched this video called *The Zombies Take Over The City*. It scared me stupid. It was all about these dead people who get out of their graves and start going to work in the city as if they were alive.

That's what my family is like in the morning. All of us. My sister Rachel's the worst. She has   20 massive shadows under her eyes. She hates going to sleep at night, that's her trouble. Mum says she always has done, ever since she was a baby. I'm getting more and more like her. I just can't get to sleep. I lie there, twisting and turning, thinking about things. After hours and hours I finally manage to drop off, and then suddenly it's morning.

We have uniform in our school. We have to wear mostly blue clothes, but we absolutely must wear   25 white shirts. I don't know why. The principal, Mrs Aske, says it's because the school has high standards. That doesn't make much sense to me. High standards of what? Blueness and whiteness?

I started pulling clothes out of my cupboard. There were no clean white shirts in there. I bundled the clothes back in and shut the door fast before they all tumbled out again.

"Mum," I called, "I can't find them."   30

"Can't find what?" said my mum, coming half-way up the stairs.

"The white shirts," I told her.

"Then they must all be in the dirty washing," she said.

"Well, what am I going to wear?"

"I don't know," she said impatiently. "Wear the one you had on yesterday."   35

"It's filthy," I told her.

"Well, I can't help that, can I?"

"Will you write me a note?"

"If I've got time," she replied, rushing back down the stairs.

I often wonder what breakfast time is like for other, normal families. In my house, there's no such thing   40 as breakfast. My dad has already left for work before I wake up. My mum doesn't seem to eat at all. Rachel walks about the house half dressed, slurping a bowl of cereal. I go downstairs and pick up an apple.

This was getting me nowhere. What was I going to do about a shirt for school? I decided I would have to wear my blue one. It was like a school shirt – just the wrong colour.

"I've got to go," Mum said, when I got downstairs. She was all dressed for work. "I've got an early   45
start. You'll be all right, won't you?"

"Yes, Mum."

"Promise you won't be late leaving the house."

"Yes, Mum."

"Rachel," she yelled up the stairs.   50

Rachel grunted in reply.

"I'm going now. Make sure you both leave in time for school."

Rachel grunted again.

"You're in charge, all right?"

Rachel grunted a third time.   55

My mum kissed me on the forehead and rushed out of the door.

"What about my note?" I shouted in desperation.

"I'll write it tomorrow," she said, slamming the door behind her.

I wouldn't even consider leaving Rachel in charge of anything. She is sixteen, so she ought to be responsible, but she isn't. She's weird. She doesn't talk to anyone for hours after she gets up. She just   60
goes around singing pop songs to herself. They all have the same tune, a sort of drone on three notes.

If a man in a black mask and a striped sweater climbed in through the window and started putting everything into a bag labelled "Loot" she wouldn't even notice. She'd go on moaning quietly to herself. Even if he asked her where the money was kept, she'd probably only grunt at him.

I ate my apple and packed my school bag.   75

Rachel had turned on the television and was watching the breakfast news. There was an item about hunting whales in the North Sea.

"I'm going now," I told her.

She was still holding her finished bowl of cereal out in front of her but she kept her eyes glued to the screen.   70

"Did you hear me?" I said.

She nodded.

"Don't you have to go in?" I asked.

She shook her head.

"How come?"   75

She tore herself away from the television. "Nothing first lesson," she said.

That was the longest sentence I had every heard her say before midday. She want back to watching whales.

"See you later then," I said.

She grunted.   80

****

I wasn't in the school five minutes before Mrs Aske grabbed me.

"What sort of a shirt is that?" she asked.

What a stupid question. What sort of a shirt did she think it was? A Martian shirt?

"It's just an ordinary shirt, miss," I said.

"It's blue."   85

"There weren't any clean ones this morning, miss," I said.

"Have you got a note?"

"No, miss."

She held out her hand. "Record book," she demanded.

I took my record book out of my bag and handed it over to her. It's a stupid little book which we have to write down our homework in and teachers can put in merit marks or debit marks. If you get three debit marks you get a detention. If you get three merit marks you don't get anything. What a fair system!

"Honestly, Matthew," Mrs Aske was saying, "look at you."

How could I look at myself without a mirror? I didn't say that, of course. I just looked at the ground.

"You look as though you have been dragged through a hedge backwards. You know standards of dress are important, Matthew."

"Sorry, miss."

I wouldn't mind if she was well-dressed. She isn't. She looks like a baked potato in a cardigan.

She handed me back my record book. "You'd better hurry along to class," she said. "You don't want to be late."

Bernie, my best friend, was waiting for me outside the classroom.

"Why are you wearing a blue shirt?" he asked.

"Because it matches my eyes," I told him.

(Adapted from Boys Don't Write Love Stories by Brian Keaney)

---

1   Spend **about 8 minutes** on this question. Use **evidence from lines 1–15** to support your answer.

How has Matthew's attitude to school changed since he was four?   [5 marks]

2   Spend **about 8 minutes** on this question. Use **evidence from lines 40–58** to support your answer.

What do you learn about Matthew's mother?   [5 marks]

3   Spend **about 15 minutes** on this question. Use **evidence from the whole passage** to support your answer.

What sort of boy do you think Matthew is?

In your answer you should refer to:
●   his thoughts about his family
●   his behaviour in school
●   and anything else you think is relevant.   [10 marks]

4   Spend **about 15 minutes** on this question. Use **evidence from the whole passage** to support your answer.

How has the writer tried to make his story enjoyable for the reader?

In your answer you should refer to:
●   the amusing incidents
●   the way the characters are presented
●   the writer's choice of words and phrases
●   and anything else you think is relevant.   [10 marks]

THE TRAIN FROM RHODESIA
by Nadine Gordimer

The train came out of the red horizon and bore down towards them over the single straight track.

The stationmaster came out of his little brick station with its pointed chalet roof, feeling the creases in his serge uniform in his legs as well. A stir of preparedness rippled through the squatting native venders waiting in the dust; the face of a carved wooden animal, eternally surprised, stuck out of a sack. The stationmaster's barefoot children wandered over. From the grey mud huts with the untidy heads that stood within a decorated mud wall, chickens, and dogs with their skin stretched like parchment over their bones, followed the children down to the track. The flushed and perspiring west cast a reflection, faint, without heat, upon the station, upon the tin shed marked 'Goods', upon the walled kraal, upon the grey tin house of the stationmaster and upon the sand, that lapped all around, from sky to sky, cast little rhythmical cups of shadow, so that the sand became the sea, and closed over the children's black feet softly and without imprint.

The stationmaster's wife sat behind the mesh of her veranda. Above her head the hunk of a sheep's carcass moved slightly, dangling in the current of air.

They waited.

The train called out, along the sky; but there was no answer; and the cry hung on: I'm coming... I'm coming...

The engine flared out now, big, whisking a dwindling body behind it; the track flared out to let it in.

Creaking, jerking, jostling, gasping, the train filled the station.

Here, let me see that one – the young woman curved her body farther out of the corridor window. Missus? smiled the old man, looking at the creatures he held in his hand. From a piece of string on his grey finger hung a tiny woven basket; he lifted it, questioning. No, no, she urged, leaning down towards him, across the height of the train towards the man in the piece of old rug; that one, that one, her hand commanded. It was a lion, carved out of soft dry wood that looked like spongecake; heraldic, black and white, with impressionistic detail burnt in. The old man held it up to her still smiling, not from the heart, but at the customer. Between its pointed teeth, in the mouth opened in an endless roar too terrible to be heard, it had a black tongue. Look, said the young husband, if you don't mind! And round the neck of the thing, a piece of fur (rat? rabbit? meerkat?); a real mane, majestic, telling you somehow that the artist had delight in the lion.

All up and down the length of the train in the dust the artists sprang, walking bent like performing animals, the better to exhibit the fantasy held towards the faces in the train. Buck, startled and stiff, staring with round black and white eyes. More lions, standing erect, grappling with strange, thin, elongated warriors who clutched spears and showed no fear in their slits of eyes. How much, they asked from the train, how much?

Give me a penny, said the little ones with nothing to sell. The dogs went and sat, quite still, under the dining car, where the train breathed out the smell of meat cooking with onion.

A man passed beneath the arch of reaching arms meeting grey-black and white in the exchange of money for staring wooden eyes, the stiff wooden legs sticking up in the air; went along under the voices and the bargaining, interrogating the wheels. Past the dogs; glancing up at the dining car where he could stare at the faces, behind glass, drinking beer, two by two, on either side of a uniform railway vase with its pale dead flower. Right to the end, to the guard's van, where the stationmaster's children had just collected their mother's two loaves of bread; to the engine itself, where the stationmaster and the driver stood talking against the steaming complaint of the resting beast.

The man called out to them, something loud and joking. They turned to laugh, in a twirl of steam. The two children careered over the sand, clutching the bread, and burst through the iron gate and up the path through the garden in which nothing grew.

Passengers drew themselves in at the corridor windows and turned into compartments to fetch money, to call someone to look. Those sitting inside looked up: suddenly different, caged faces, boxed in, cut off after the contact outside. There was an orange a child would like... What about the chocolate? It wasn't very nice...

A girl had collected a handful of the hard kind, that no one liked, out of the chocolate box, and was throwing them out of the dining car to the dogs. But the hens darted in and swallowed the chocolates, incredibly quick and accurate, before they had even dropped in the dust, and the dogs, a little bewildered, looked up with their brown eyes, not expecting anything.

– No, leave it, said the young woman, don't take it...

Too expensive, too much, she shook her head and raised her voice to the old man, giving up the lion. He held it high where she had handed it to him. No, she said, shaking her head. Three-and-six? insisted her husband loudly. Yes baas! laughed the old man. *Three-and-six?* – the young man was incredulous. Oh leave it – she said. The young man stopped. Don't you want it? he said, keeping his face close to the old man. No, never mind, she said, leave it. The old native kept his head on one side, looking at them sideways, holding the lion. Three-and-six, he murmured, as old people repeat things to themselves.

The young woman drew her head in. She went into the coupé and sat down. Out of the window, on the other side, there was nothing; sand and bush, a thorn tree. Back through the open doorway, past the figure of her husband in the corridor, there was the station, the voices, wooden animals waving, running feet. Her eye followed the funny little valance of scrolled wood that outlined the chalet roof of the station; she thought of the lion and smiled. That bit of fur round the neck. But the wooden buck, the hippos, the elephants, the baskets that already bulked out of their brown paper under the seat and on the luggage rack! How will they look at home? Where will you put them? What will they mean away from the places you found them? Away from the unreality of the last few weeks? The young man outside. But he is not part of the unreality; he is for good now. Odd... somewhere there was an idea that he, that living with him, was part of the holiday, the strange places.

Outside, a bell rang. The stationmaster was leaning against the end of the train, green flag rolled in readiness. A few men who had got down to stretch their legs sprang on to the train, clinging to the observation platforms, or perhaps merely standing on the iron step, holding the rail; but on the train, safe from the one dusty platform, the one tin house, the empty sand.

There was a grunt. The train jerked. Through the glass the beer drinkers looked out, as if they could not see beyond it. Behind the flyscreen, the stationmaster's wife sat facing back at them beneath the darkening hunk of meat.

There was a shout. The flag drooped out. Joints not yet coordinated, the segmented body of the train heaved and bumped back against itself. It began to move; slowly the scrolled chalet moved past it, the yells of the natives, running alongside, jetted up into the air, fell back at different levels. Staring wooden faces waved drunkenly, there, then gone, questioning for the last time at the windows. Here, one-and-six bass! – As one automatically opens a hand to catch a thrown ball, a man fumbled wildly down his pocket, brought up the shilling and sixpence and threw them out; the old native, gasping, his skinny toes splaying the sand, flung the lion.

The children were waving, the dogs stood, tails uncertain, watching the train go: past the mud huts, where a woman turned to look up from the smoke of the fire, her hand pausing on her hip.

The stationmaster went slowly in under the chalet.

The old native stood, breath blowing out the skin between his ribs, feet tense, balanced in the sand, smiling and shaking his head. In his opened palm, held in the attitude of receiving, was the retrieved shilling and sixpence.

The blind end of the train was being pulled helplessly out of the station.

The young man swung in from the corridor, breathless. He was shaking his head with laughter and triumph. Here! he said. And waggled the lion at her. One-and-six!

What? she said.

He laughed. I was arguing with him for fun, bargaining – when the train had pulled out already, he came tearing after ... One-and-six Baas! So there's your lion.

She was holding it away from her, the head with the open jaws, the pointed teeth, the black tongue, the wonderful ruff of fur facing her. She was looking at it with an expression of not seeing, of seeing something different. Her face was drawn up, wryly, like the face of a discomforted child. Her mouth lifted nervously at the corner. Very slowly, cautious, she lifted her finger and touched the mane, where it was joined to the wood.

But how could you, she said. He was shocked by the dismay of her face.

Good Lord, he said, what's the matter?

If you wanted the thing, she said, her voice rising and breaking with the shrill impotence of anger, why didn't you buy it in the first place? If you wanted it, why didn't you pay for it? Why didn't you take it decently, when he offered it? Why did you have to wait for him to run after the train with it, and give him one-and-six! One-and-six!

She was pushing it at him, trying to force him to take the lion. He stood astonished, his hands hanging at his sides.

But you wanted it! You liked it so much?

– It's a beautiful piece of work, she said fiercely, as if to protect it from him.

You liked it so much! You said yourself it was too expensive –

Oh *you* – she said, hopeless and furious. *You* … She threw the lion onto the seat.

He stood looking at her.

She sat down again in the corner and, her face slumped in her hands, stared out of the window. Everything was turning round inside her. One-and-six. One-and-six. One-and-six for the wood and the carving and the sinews of the legs and the switch of the tail. The mouth open like that and the teeth. The black tongue, rolling, like a wave. The mane round the neck. To give one-and-six for that. The heat of shame mounted through her legs and body and sounded in her ears like the sound of sand pouring. Pouring, pouring. She sat there, sick. A weariness, a tastelessness, the discovery of a void made her hands slacken their grip, atrophy, atrophy emptily, as if the hour was not worth their grasp. She was feeling like this again. She had thought it was something to do with singleness, with being alone and belonging too much to oneself.

She sat there not wanting to move or speak, or to look at anything even; so that the mood should be associated with nothing, no object, word or sight that might recur and so recall the feeling again … Smuts blew in grittily, settled on her hand. Her back remained at exactly the same angle, turned against the young man sitting with his hands drooping between his sprawled legs, and the lion, fallen on its side in the corner.

The train had cast the station like a skin. It called out to the sky, I'm coming, I'm coming; and again, there was no answer.

From *Selected Stories*, Nadine Gordimer published by Jonathan Cape

Explain the various ways in which the story contrasts the worlds inside and outside the train, and show how far this contrast helps to explain why the young woman finally rejects the carving.

Support your answer by referring to and quoting from the story.

Remember to put quotation marks round any words or phrases from the story that you have used.

[20 marks]

Gillian Clarke

No Hands

War-planes have been at it all day long
shaking the world, strung air
humming like pianos when children bang the keys

over and over; willow warbler song
5 and jet planes; lads high on speed up there
in a mindless thrum; down here a brake of trees

churns to a rolling wave and there's no let
in the after-quiver along air-waves struck
by silly boys who think they strum guitars,

10 who skim the fields like surfboards over crests
of hedges, where a tractor swims in a green wake
of grass dust tossed to dry under sun and stars:

boy scaring boy off the face of his own land,
all do and dare, and look at me, no hands.

Jac Codi Baw

They have torn down in the space of time
it takes to fill a shopping bag,
the building that stood beside my car.
It was grown over with ragwort,
5 toadflax and buddleia, windows
blind with boarding. Other cars
had time to drive away. Mine
is splattered with the stone's blood, smoky
with ghosts. We are used to the slow
10 change that weather brings, the gradual
death of a generation, old bricks
crumbling. Inside the car dust lies,
grit in my eyes, in my hair.

He doesn't care. It's a joke to him
15 clearing space for the pile-drivers,
cheerful in his yellow machine,
cat-calling, laughing at my grief.
But for him too the hand-writing
of a city will be erased.
20 I can't laugh. Too much comes down
in the deaths of warehouses. Brickdust,
shards of Caernarfon slate. Blood on our hands.

What criticisms does Clarke seem to be making of the pilots in 'No Hands' and of the JCB driver in 'Jac Codi Baw'?

How does she make clear her feelings about them? [27 marks]

THE GOING OF THE BATTERY
WIVES' LAMENT
(*November 2, 1899*)

I

O IT was sad enough, weak enough, mad enough –
Light in their loving as soldiers can be –
First to risk choosing them, leave alone losing them
Now, in far battle, beyond the South Sea!...

II

– Rain came down drenchingly; but we unblenchingly
Trudged on beside them through mirk and through mire,
They stepping steadily – only too readily! –
Scarce as if stepping brought parting-time nigher.

III

Great guns were gleaming there, living things seeming there,
Cloaked in their tar-cloths, upmouthed to the night;
Wheels wet and yellow from axle to felloe,
Throats blank of sound, but prophetic to sight.

IV

Gas-glimmers drearily, blearily, eerily
Lit our pale faces outstretched for one kiss,
While we stood prest to them, with a last quest to them
Not to court perils that honour could miss.

V

Sharp were those sighs of ours, blinded these eyes of ours,
When at last moved away under the arch
All we loved. Aid for them each woman prayed for them,
Treading back slowly the track of their march.

VI

Some one said: "Nevermore will they come: evermore
Are they now lost to us." O it was wrong!
Though may be hard their ways, some Hand will guard their ways,
Bear them through safely, in brief time or long.

VII

– Yet, voices haunting us, daunting us, taunting us,
Hint in the night-time when life beats are low
Other and graver things … Hold we to braver things,
Wait we, in trust, what Time's fulness shall show.

Look at the poem *The Going of the Battery* by Thomas Hardy.

Describe the scene of the soldiers leaving for war and explain how the wives feel.

Give examples of how the language is used to:
- build up the picture of the scene
- show the wives' feelings.

[20 marks]

Look at the letter below.

1 Make a list of the criticisms the letter makes of the National Lottery.　　　[10 marks]

2 How does the writer of the letter try to influence your thoughts and feelings about the way the National Lottery is run?

In your answer comment on:
- how the writer uses facts and opinions;
- the writer's choice of language;
- the different ways the writer tries to persuade you.　　　[10 marks]

The National Lottery is operated by a company called Camelot. Some people disagree with the way the Lottery is run. The letter below was printed in a daily newspaper.

The Vicarage,
Mill Street,
PENRITH,
Cumbria.
CA7 5BU

The Editor,
The Daily Recorder,
Recorder House,
LONDON.
EC1 2DD

Dear Sir,

On Saturday night there will be an estimated rollover jackpot of £40 million – the biggest ever seen in this country. Isn't that good news? you may ask. Well, I have to disagree. The Lottery could have been set up in such a way that a £40 million jackpot could be spread among 40 people, each receiving £1 million, or even 400 people receiving one hundred thousand pounds apiece. After all, one hundred thousand pounds would change most people's lives for the better and £1 million would transform them.

But the Lottery is not about making people happy – it is a business set up to make its shareholders rich. And the best way to sell its goods – its tickets – is to advertise them with a prize so vast it creates huge publicity. This sucks in millions of people, in particular those who can least afford to buy the tickets.

That is why I say that this Saturday's rollover jackpot is obscene. I'm not against a harmless flutter but the Bible does say that "the love of money is the root of all evil". And this is what these inflated prizes are encouraging: sheer greed. Of course we can all be helped by receiving extra sums of money. Only a fool would deny that. But that is totally different from suddenly winning the ridiculously high amounts of the current jackpots.

On average people spend £2 a week on the National Lottery. What this really means is that some, like me, don't take part at all, but others hand over far more than £2. A reasonably well-off person can spend £5 or more each week without noticing, but a poor person can't afford to do that.

Unfortunately there is evidence that a minority of the less well off are gambling on the Lottery with more money than they can afford. As a result, there will be homes next week with less to spend on the essentials of food and clothing. There is also now evidence of an increase in addictive gambling. This week a charity set up to help those who cannot control their gambling, Gamblers Anonymous, announced that calls for help are up nearly 20 per cent since the National Lottery began. Despite this, Camelot changes nothing. For them, the only thing that matters is the size of the vast profit it makes – more than £1 million a week.

We are fed comments from them about the amount the National Lottery raises for good causes. Do not be fooled. Far too little of the huge takings each week – a measly 28 per cent – goes to 'good causes'. And even less goes to actual charities. The National Lottery is in fact taking money away from charities because people are encouraged to spend money on it which otherwise they might have given to a charity.

In short, the National Lottery has turned out to be neither the boost to charity it was promised to be, nor the harmless form of entertainment the Government predicted.

Yours faithfully,
Reverend D. Williams

Question 6

(a) **Read Item 1, the article *How Many Young People are Homeless?***

    (i)   According to the article, what are the different reasons young people become homeless? (4)

    (ii)   Explain in your own words why The Children Act 1989 has not solved the problems of homeless young people. (6)

(b) **Read Item 2, the leaflet from The Salvation Army.**

    (i)   List the different ways in which the Salvation Army helps people like Jim. (8)

    (ii)   Explain how the Salvation Army uses language to get its message across in **each of** the following three extracts:

        (A)   "Once on the street, homeless people become prey to all sorts of illnesses, all potential killers. In fact, over 600 people a year die on the streets."

        (B)   "With your generosity we can give vulnerable people not only a happier Christmas but a brighter future too. People like Jim."

        (C)   "We are the ones to lend a sympathetic ear, the ones with the comforting arm, the ones offering true friendship and support during difficult times." (6)

(c) These two items about homelessness are very different.

    Compare Item 1, the article, with Item 2, the leaflet.

    You should write about:

- what they contain
- how the material is presented
- the language they use. (30)

[54 marks]

Item 1

This is an extract from a newspaper article which provides information about homeless young people.

HOW MANY YOUNG PEOPLE ARE HOMELESS?

In recent times, reports have suggested:

- more young people are becoming homeless
- more young people are sleeping rough
- more and more homeless young people have no job.

YOUTH EMPLOYMENT AND PAY

Often, young people are trapped. They cannot escape from homelessness and unemployment. Without work, it is difficult to find a place to live; but it is almost impossible to get a job without a permanent address.

In 1995, a survey found that approximately one in five 16–19 year old men and one in six 16–19 year old women were unemployed. Many of those who had jobs worked part-time; many received low wages; and many jobs did not last for long.

Such problems can make it difficult to get a home.

LEAVING CARE WITH NOWHERE TO GO

Some young people are not brought up by their parents. They are brought up in care, in homes run by the local authorities. When they leave this care, they have little or no support from family and friends. They cannot occasionally return 'home' to be looked after.

Often, they have to cope on their own straight away. They might have had no advice on how to manage money and how to look after themselves properly.

The Children Act 1989 tries to help. It says social services departments must help youngsters leaving care until they are 21. However, there is a lack of money, so many young people are given no help at all.

They may be left to find their own place to live. This can be difficult and the young people can end up living in areas they do not know, or in temporary accommodation. Sometimes, a young person cannot manage, loses the home and becomes homeless.

In one survey, 60 per cent of under 18 year olds said they would need help with housekeeping and the control of their money if they were living alone. Sadly, this support tends to be lacking.

BEING FORCED TO LEAVE HOME

The government says that homelessness is often caused by the fact that friends and family can not – or will not – provide a home for a young person.

In 1995, 86 per cent of people who had recently become homeless said they had been forced to leave home. They blamed family arguments, eviction or abuse. Another 7 per cent left because of overcrowding.

This is part of a leaflet issued by The Salvation Army at Christmas describing its work with homeless people and asking for contributions to enable The Salvation Army to continue its work.

If you're sleeping rough you dread a clear night sky.

For homeless people a star-filled sky can be deadly. Without the few degrees of extra warmth that a blanket of cloud provides, the temperature plummets dangerously.

Many homeless people are blameless for their situation: unemployment and home repossessions are just two causes. Once on the street, homeless people become prey to all sorts of illnesses, all potential killers. In fact, over 600 people a year die on the streets.

Without anyone to care about them, those living rough feel lonely and hopeless. Especially at this time of year when most people are making plans with their family to come home for Christmas.

But The Salvation Army cares. We are the largest provider of accommodation for single homeless people all year round. We have also developed a successful programme for helping them find a permanent home off the streets.

With your generosity we can give vulnerable people not only a happier Christmas but a brighter future too. People like Jim.

Make this Christmas the start of a new life for Jim.

Home for Jim was on a windswept hill amongst some brambles.

His dearest wish was to make a fresh start. He saw advertised what he thought was the perfect job – a live-in kitchen hand at a local hotel.

Jim spruced himself up as best he could and set off on the two-mile walk for the interview, full of excitement, positive his luck was about to change.

However, his spirits were soon dashed. The interviewer took one look at his crumpled clothes and unshaven face and told Jim curtly, 'Sorry, the job's gone.' What he didn't see was the hope fade from Jim's eyes.

Weak from hunger, the walk back up the hill seemed a lot longer than it had a couple of hours earlier.

It was shortly after this that our local Salvation Army centre heard about Jim. Armed with a flask of soup an officer visited him, listening sympathetically to his story.

Even at this low point Jim still had the spirit to make this wry comment: 'I can't really blame the bloke at the hotel - sleeping rough doesn't exactly keep the creases in your trousers!'

Jim went back with the officer to The Salvation Army hostel where he enjoyed a hot bath, a close shave, a change of clothes, a

wholesome meal, friendship and, finally, a comfortable bed.

He's still staying at the local Salvation Army hostel, building up his confidence with the help of dedicated, caring officers. Jim's determined to get himself a job and we're sure that with your help the New Year can bring a new life for him.

The Guiding Star Appeal will bring hope to many homeless people

By supporting the Guiding Star Appeal you will help us to make sure that no one spends Christmas fighting the cold and hunger out on the streets. You can show them there is real hope for the future.

To many we are a second family to replace the one they have lost touch with. We are the ones to lend a sympathetic ear, the ones with the comforting arm, the ones offering true friendship and support during difficult times.

Your help now means we can continue our vital work with homeless people. A gift from you could give someone a new reason for living. Please help us make sure that we can welcome those with no one else to turn to this Christmas.

In an extended piece of writing, present your views on the following subject:

Do you believe it is right to keep animals?

Think carefully about the issues below as you prepare to write about this topic.

Pets

– the health risk
– the problem of strays
– the benefits for young and old

Zoos and Safari Parks

– their educational value
– they help preserve endangered species
– the unnatural surroundings

KEEPING ANIMALS

Farms

– a source of quality food
– farmers keep their animals healthy
– animals kept in cramped conditions

Animals as Entertainment

– circus animals forced to perform tricks
– harmless fun

Any other ideas of your own?

[30 marks]

Question 2

Describe one of the following in such a way that it can be easily imagined by your reader:

- a city at night
- a deserted beach
- a busy shopping centre.

[54 marks]

Question 3

Your local council has plans for a large-scale housing development and some of the local countryside may have to go. As a member of the council, write the words of a speech either supporting or opposing these plans.

[20 marks]

Question 4

Write a story about a time when you felt you were treated unfairly.

[20 marks]

READING Question 1

This question was based on a passage which you would not have seen before the exam. My comments remind you how to look for clues in a passage, and how to answer the questions in ways which will gain you high marks. These answers are at Grade A. Compare your own answers with them.

Matthew used to like school – according to his mother he "loved" it, and there is a photograph of him on his first day at school, looking really happy ("with a great big grin on his face"). Now, he can hardly believe it. He thinks of "little kids" as "suckers", in other words, he thinks that they are easily taken in by adults (certainly where school is concerned, and perhaps about other things as well), and he feels very resentful towards whoever it was ("some wise-guy") he imagines inventing school back in the Middle Ages. However, there is humour underlying all that Matthew says, and although he dislikes some things about school, there are aspects of it which he probably quite likes.

Examiner's Comments

Five marks are available for this question. Two would certainly have been gained by explaining what Matthew's attitude towards school **was** and what it **is** now, and at least one mark would be given for **quoting some textual evidence** to support that. Another mark would be awarded for a **reference to Matthew's complaint** about the man who invented school, and the fifth mark might be given for a **quotation** in support of that. To be really sure of the final mark, however, it's a good idea, even with a straightforward question like this, to show that you can **read between the lines** – which is why this answer included the comment about Matthew's sense of humour.

In lines 40–58 we learn that Matthew's mother seems more involved in her work than in looking after her family. She isn't interested in breakfast (in fact, Matthew comments that she "doesn't seem to eat at all"), and hurries off for "an early start" assuming that Matthew and Rachel can get themselves off to school. She leaves Rachel in charge, even though

Rachel is not "responsible" in Matthew's eyes, and she cannot make the time to write a note about Matthew's shirt, even though she hasn't made sure there was a clean one for him to wear to school. She does show Matthew some affection by kissing him before she goes, but she seems to be in a constant state of being disorganised and in a hurry, as she "rushed out of the door … slamming [it] behind her".

Examiner's Comments

The marks here would be awarded for **general comments** about the mother's attitudes and behaviour and **supporting quotations**. Additional marks would be gained for **specific examples**, such as mentions of breakfast, the shirt and the note. Once again, you have to show that you can **read between the lines**, which is what the last sentence of the answer does. This answer also shows **good use of quotations** by integrating them into sentences rather than setting them out separately. Note how the final quotation has been correctly amended and punctuated to fit the sentence.

3

Matthew seems to be a thoughtful and mature boy with a good sense of humour. Despite his mother's interest in work and his sister's lack of communication early in the morning, he tries to talk to them both and does not lose his temper, although he shows some "desperation" when his mother leaves without writing him a note. His humour comes over when he thinks of his family in connection with a horror film about zombies, when he suggests that Rachel wouldn't notice a comic-strip burglar under her nose, and when he wonders why the colour of a school shirt makes a difference to "high standards". However, when the teacher tells him off, he keeps quiet ("I didn't say that, of course") and is polite to her even though he is longing to answer back. His humour comes out again when he tells Bernie that he is wearing a wrong-coloured shirt because it matches his eyes. Perhaps Matthew is actually a little unhappy beneath the surface: he doesn't want to admit to his best friend that his family is disorganised, and we know that he doesn't sleep well. It is also possible that he is genuinely concerned about the other members of his family – he doesn't appear to see much of his father, his mother is always in a rush and doesn't eat properly, and he is worried that he is becoming more like his sister.

Examiner's Comments

It is good to start the answer with a **firm opening statement** which is then **developed in detail**. The references to how Matthew reacts to Rachel, his mother, the teacher and Bernie all support the first sentence through a **combination of direct quotations and detailed references**. This answer has taken the hint from the third bullet point to **broaden comments** about Matthew, using the evidence of the text to **speculate – but to stay with the evidence** as the last sentence of the answer does. Note that, as **this question is worth 10 marks** rather than 5, **this answer is longer and more detailed** than those to questions 1 and 2.

The writer has made this passage enjoyable through the use of humour. Some of the humour is based on incidents or actions, such as Matthew rushing around looking for a shirt while his mother is unconcerned and his sister slouches around apparently unaware of much at all, but being left "in charge" by her mother. Other humour is verbal – Matthew's comments about his "goofy" younger self, the "wise-guy" who invented school, use of words like "slurping" and "grunting" to describe Rachel, his comments about Mrs Aske looking like a "baked potato in a cardigan" and his reply to Bernie at the end. All the characters are seen through Matthew's eyes, which means that they all have humorous aspects, but the writer does convey a serious point underneath. We feel that Matthew worries about his family life, and a serious point is raised about Mrs Aske, uniform and "standards" – this topic appeals to teenage readers because it is close to their experience and they will probably have strong views about it like Matthew. The whole setting of this passage will probably appeal to them because they will recognise themselves and their families, or other families they know, in the description. Finally, because Matthew speaks directly to the reader and because he has a good sense of humour, the passage is involving and appealing.

Examiner's Comments

A question which requires a **wide-ranging reaction to the whole passage** needs careful planning. This answer has **combined the first and third bullet points**, as so much of the humour comes from the language. This shows a **good overview** of the passage. The answer has used the hint given in the third bullet point to write two

excellent concluding sentences which sum up the appeal of the passage. Once again, the answer includes **appropriate details and quotations** to support the claims.

READING: Question 2

Where you have been given pre-release material to study, you may be asked one large-scale question which requires a long and detailed answer rather than several focused questions requiring shorter answers. This model answer shows how to write well in response to a question about a complete short story which you will have read and thought about before the exam. This is an A Grade answer. Compare your own answer with it.

> The whole point of this story is to show how the contrast between the worlds inside and outside the train affects the young woman and makes her think about the carved lion, and her relationship with her husband, very differently as a result of her experience at the station.
>
> The opening description sets the scene of the world outside the train: the "native vendors" who rely on selling souvenirs to travellers to make some money; their poverty is suggested by the hungry dogs "with their skin stretched like parchment over their bones", the "barefoot children" and the dust, rather than soil, which forms the earth. There is a contrast even here, however: the stationmaster has a "serge uniform", and his wife is able to sit "behind the mesh of her veranda", with a sheep's carcass hanging nearby ready to provide food, so although the local inhabitants are all poor compared with the travellers, some are better-off than others. Even in this lowly world, you can still be at the bottom of the pile.
>
> The description of the train emphasises how it is a stranger to its surroundings. It is described almost like an invader, in some ways welcome because it brings the possibility of trade (so "the track flared out <u>to let it in</u>"), but perhaps also resented because it represents a privileged existence denied to the natives. At the very end of the story we are told that the train "had cast the station like a skin" which suggests that its stopping place is now a forgotten or rejected piece of its past. At both the beginning and end of the story when it sounds as though the train is calling out "I'm coming … I'm coming …" there is no answer – the world around it does not really accept it or want it.

In addition to the contrast in descriptions of the worlds inside and outside the train, the gap between them is symbolised by how the young woman leans down towards the native selling the lion, "across the height of the train towards the man" – the bodywork of the carriage literally and symbolically keeps them apart and makes it difficult for them to make contact with each other. When the passengers "drew themselves in at the corridor windows and turned into compartments to fetch money" they are again literally and symbolically turning their backs on the poor natives and returning to their own privileged world. To the people in the train, the natives are "artists" and a "fantasy" – they are not real people struggling to make a living, but are romanticised on the one hand and patronised on the other, as when the husband thinks he has been clever by getting the carved lion for a much lower price than was first demanded, or when the young woman's hand gesture "commanded" the carving she wished to be shown.

Inside the train, separated by glass from the reality of the outside world, passengers are sitting comfortably, "drinking beer" in the dining car "on either side of a uniform railway vase with its pale dead flower". The flower is dead because it cannot survive in this unreal world of luxury and privilege. The story goes on to say explicitly that the passengers inside the train were "different, caged faces, boxed in, cut off after the contact outside". They have oranges and chocolate, which they are willing to give away because "it wasn't very nice", not out of a genuine wish to share it. Even then, they throw the chocolate to the dogs rather than offer it to the children.

All of this builds up in the young woman's mind so that she gradually realises how unreal the situation is: holiday souvenirs are not so important and are not what life is actually about – and are her feelings towards her husband as unreal as her longing for a souvenir?

"Odd … somewhere there was an idea that he, that living with him, was part of the holiday, the strange places."

This is why she finally rejects the carving. It now represents to her the "blindness" of the train and its limited, unseeing community of travellers which she contrasts with the harsh realities of life for the native villagers. To her husband, the carved lion is just something she wanted which he managed to get at a knock-down price and he can't understand why she has suddenly become so "hopeless and furious". She is hopeless, because she realises the gulf, the "void", between the two cultures and her inability to do anything about it. She is furious because he cannot even see there is a problem. So she ends up with her back turned towards her husband, trying to forget both him and the situation, but being reminded of the unpleasantness by the "smuts" from the engine which are "grittily" settling on her hand, the hand out of which she has just thrown the lion in an attempt to reject what it stands for.

Examiner's Comments

This is a **full and detailed answer** which shows good understanding of the story on different levels, for example **literal and symbolic meanings**. It has **linked different parts of the text**, for example the references to the repeated description of the noise made by the train at the beginning and the end, which shows a **good overview**. It has **integrated brief quotations** within the writing, but has set out separately one **longer quotation which is central to the candidate's interpretation** of the story.

This answer has **kept to the question** and has avoided the temptation, for example, to write about the carving itself. The reference to the social status of the stationmaster and his wife could have led to irrelevance, but the brief comment made is useful in establishing just how poor and lowly the souvenir-sellers are.

The answer has an **introduction which states clearly how the candidate's understanding of the story relates to the task**, and a **conclusion which skilfully uses words from the text to explain and emphasise the interpretation** of it. The answer is of very high quality and would gain full marks. **Responses to pre-release material are expected to show that you have thought at length about the text and can make a sophisticated, supported response** to tasks set on it.

READING: Question 3

This is another answer to pre-release material, requiring comparison of two poems. In some ways this is easier than writing about a short story, because there is less text to deal with. On the other hand, you will be expected to make perceptive, extended comments about the poet's ideas and techniques. This is an A Grade answer. Compare your own answer with it.

In both of these poems, Gillian Clarke is criticising people. In "No Hands" she is saying that the pilots are childish, silly and big-headed, while in "Jac Codi Baw" she makes the JCB driver seem almost like a murderer who takes pleasure in his evil deeds. I shall look in detail at how she makes these feelings clear to her readers.

The pilots are first made to seem like children having tantrums; the noise their planes make is compared to

> " … pianos when children bang the keys
> over and over".

Clarke goes on to suggest that the pilots seem drunk, as they are "high on speed": this could mean that they get a kick from flying so fast or it could even be a pun on "speed", suggesting that the pilots behave as though they are drugged and unaware of what they are doing.

She thinks the pilots are immature, and conveys this by using words such as "lads" and "silly boys" to describe them – these words continue the image of spoilt children from the earlier part of the poem. This idea is strengthened by the reference to "surfboards", which has associations of lazing around, having a good time, perhaps being young and irresponsible and so on, so Clarke really denies the skill and training the pilots need to fly their planes.

In the last two lines, Clarke uses the word "boy" twice, once in a dismissive way to describe the pilots again but the second time to describe a farm labourer driving his tractor in the fields below the aircraft, to make him seem vulnerable and threatened by these war-machines. The last line is really contemptuous towards the pilots, making them out to be boastful, shallow and stupid, like a child riding a bike dangerously in a way that could result in an accident:

> "all do and dare, and look at me, no hands."

The structure of this poem, as well as the words and ideas, is used to emphasise Clarke's feelings of anger towards the pilots. The poem is a sonnet, set out in traditional style as four three-line stanzas and a final couplet. A sonnet is traditionally a love poem, and so the use of this form adds to the irony of Clarke's message in the poem, which is nothing like love. The final couplet of a sonnet traditionally sums up its central idea: here, the lines makes the pilots seem really childish and stupid.

In "Jac Codi Baw", Clarke expresses equally strong feelings about the JCB driver who "doesn't care" about tearing down an old building – "It's a joke to him".

Clarke describes the attractive qualities of the building before it was demolished, and uses this to make the reader feel sad that it has gone, before she puts any ideas straight into the reader's mind as she did in "No Hands":

> "It was grown over with ragwort,
> toadflax and buddleia…"

The only clue the reader has at this point about Clarke's feelings is the use of the words "torn down" to describe the demolition of the building.

Whereas the images used in "No Hands" were to do with children and games, the imagery in "Jac Codi Baw" is more violent. Clarke compares the demolition of the building to the death of a living thing, and so she refers to "the stone's blood" and "the death of warehouses' which leaves "Blood on our hands".

As in "No Hands", Clarke sets up a contrast. In the first poem it was between the fighter pilots and the farmhand. In "Jac Codi Baw" it is between the attitudes of the poet and the JCB driver, who is "cat-calling, laughing at my grief". In one line, Clarke describes him in a similar way to the pilots in "No Hands", belittling him by describing him as "cheerful in his yellow machine": this makes him seem like a little boy with a toy, not understanding (or not caring about) what he is doing.

Both of these poems convey deeply-felt criticisms of the pilots and the JCB driver. Strangely, perhaps, "Jac Codi Baw" contains more violent language and imagery than "No Hands", even though it is about a building being demolished rather than being about machines which could cause multiple human deaths. That is perhaps because of Clarke's chosen approach: she tries to deal with her feelings about the pilots and their planes by belittling them, whereas she tries to make people see how important buildings are by personifying them.

Both approaches are unusual, but very successful in conveying the strength of her feelings and her criticisms of the pilots and the JCB driver.

Examiner's Comments

This answer **works methodically through the texts, using quotations effectively** to illustrate points. It shows **appreciation of the poet's feelings, attitudes and ideas** and these have been explored in some detail. The **close textual analysis** includes some **consideration of the structure of the first poem** and how this is used to contribute to its meaning. Most important of all, the answer makes **comparisons and contrasts** between the two texts wherever possible, and has used this approach to illustrate Clarke's originality, showing a **genuine personal response** to the poems.

READING: Question 4

This example of a question on pre-release material uses a pre-1900 poem. It provides help through a clearly-structured task. This question was set on a Foundation Tier paper; the following answer is therefore at Grade C level, which is the highest grade available for this paper. Compare your answer with it.

The scene is soldiers leaving for a distant war. It is dark and it has been raining. The wives are sad that the men are leaving, worried that they may not return safely, but try not to show it. They pray that all will be well, but they don't feel too sure about it.

Hardy uses language to build up a picture of the scene and to emphasise the emotions that are felt by both the soldiers and their wives. The weather is bad ("rain came down drenchingly") and everywhere is dark and muddy ("through murk and through mire"), so that even the wheels of the great guns are "yellow" with clay and mud. There is some feeble light ("gas-glimmers drearily") which makes the weapons shine in the dark and shows the women's "pale faces"; perhaps they feel even worse about the dangers facing their husbands when they can see the guns so clearly. All of these details contribute to the sadness of the scene, and Hardy uses different techniques to emphasise the effect, for example alliteration to link words across stanzas ("great guns gleaming … gas-glimmers") and repetition and internal rhyme in lines to build up a sense of the scene and the feelings of the women as they think back to how they first became involved with the soldiers ("sad enough, weak enough, mad enough").

At the start of the poem the women's worries are expressed through the same device of repetition and internal rhyme:

"First to risk choosing them, leave alone losing them".

Later, they hope that God will protect the soldiers, praying that "some Hand will guard their ways" – the capital H shows that God is meant by this word. Their inner fears are shown by Hardy's use of triple internal rhyme to link words which show that the wives feel worry, despair and helplessness when they remember the sounds of their husbands' voices after they've gone:

"Yet, voices haunting us, daunting us, taunting us".

They fear that they may not see their loved-ones again, and Hardy uses speech to add to the impact of their concern, as though we can hear what the women are saying ("Nevermore will they come: evermore are they now lost to us"). They feel that all they can do is wait and hope for the best. They now seem to think more about fate ("Time") than about God, but the ending of the poem is resigned rather than sad, as though the women are determined to put a brave face on for the sake of their husbands:

"Hold we to braver things,
Wait we, in trust, what Time's fullness shall show."

Examiner's Comments

This answer covers the task well. There is a **brief introduction which sets out the general response** and then **each of the bullet points** is answered in turn. This has made it easy for the candidate to keep on task and to choose **a range of apt quotations and references** to support the points made. There are some **effective comments on Hardy's techniques**, because they have been **explained as well as identified**. The answer shows a **good appreciation of the tone** of the poem – particularly how the wives' feelings change – and also shows a **sympathetic personal engagement** with the text.

This question on a non-fiction text (here, a letter) requires you to complete two different tasks, one of which is a straightforward listing exercise and one which requires you to show your skill in identifying and describing persuasive techniques. Although equal marks are offered for both parts of the question, the listing is much more straightforward and you should approach this as an opportunity both to 'get some marks in the bank' and to get 'inside' the text in preparation for the more demanding second task. These answers are at Grade A. Compare your answers with them.

The criticisms the letter makes of the National Lottery are:

- rollover jackpots give too much money to one individual;
- more people could benefit from smaller wins;
- the real purpose of the National Lottery is to make its shareholders rich;
- it encourages people who cannot afford it to buy tickets in the hope of a big win;
- it encourages greed;
- there is evidence that some people are unable to spend on necessities such as food and clothing because of what they spend on the National Lottery;
- there has been an increase in addictive gambling since the National Lottery began;
- only a fairly small proportion of National Lottery takings goes to "good causes";
- even less money goes to charities;
- in fact, the National Lottery is taking money away from charities because people are spending what they might have given to charities on National Lottery tickets.

Examiner's Comments

As there are 10 marks for this question, the candidate has been **wise to find and list 10 points**. In a listing question, it is perfectly **acceptable to use bullet points** or a numbered list if you prefer (but take care not to get in a muddle with question numbers!). In a listing question, **you do not need to worry about using your own words** unless the question tells you to. Here, the candidate has made sensible use of words from the original with some paraphrasing to keep the answers brief. It is **not absolutely necessary to**

put an introductory statement before the ten points as has been done here, but it does give a good impression to the examiner – it suggests that you are concerned about the appearance and clarity of your work.

The writer uses a number of ways to try and influence the reader's thoughts and feelings about the way the National Lottery is run.

First, he uses a number of facts – or, in this case, figures – to support his case. For instance, he mentions the value of one particular rollover jackpot (£40 million), the average amount spent by individuals on National Lottery tickets each week (£2), the increase in the number of calls to Gamblers Anonymous (nearly 20%) since the National Lottery began, and the proportion of the National Lottery takings which go to "good causes" (28%). These facts are used to show either how <u>much</u> there is a problem (in the first three cases) or (in the last case) how <u>little</u> money actually goes to "good causes".

In among these facts and figures are a number of opinions intended to sweep along the unquestioning reader. For example, the writer comments on the extent to which winning certain sums of money would change people's lives: that may be true, but there is no way of proving it, and it would not necessarily be true for people who are already very rich. He also states what the purpose of the National lottery is – "to make its shareholders rich". Those shareholders, and no doubt the Camelot organisation, might well dispute that, as they would probably argue against the idea that they use prize money to "suck in millions of people". It is the writer's opinion that people who take part in the National Lottery are motivated by greed, and that certain groups of people can or cannot afford to spend so much per week on tickets.

While the writer says there is evidence to support his claim that some families are going without food and clothes in order to buy Lottery tickets, he does not quote the actual evidence, or the source where it might be found. His comments about the amount of money going to charities are similarly unsupported and unreferenced. The final paragraph of the letter is a pure statement of opinion.

The writer employs some powerful language to try and influence the reader. Words and phrases such as "sucks in", "obscene", "sheer greed", "ridiculously high amounts", "vast profit", "measly 28%" are intended to work on the reader's emotions so that he or she is swept along by the implications of the language and inevitably agrees with the writer.

In addition to the mix of fact and opinion and the use of emotive language, the writer uses some other techniques to influence the reader's thoughts and feelings. For example, there is a rhetorical question near the start ("Isn't that good news?") which draws readers into the argument and makes them think about what their answer would be. The use of words and phrases such as "Well" and "After all" to start sentences makes the tone sound reasonable and chatty, almost as if it were a friend talking to you. By saying "I'm not against a harmless flutter", the writer tries to appear ordinary and reasonable, not like a crusader on a mission, and his admission that winning money can be very pleasant reinforces this image. He also varies the structure and length of his sentences for effect, for example "And even less goes to actual charities" stands out from the sentence on either side of it. The final sentence is carefully balanced around a "neither … nor" structure, so that it sounds like a reasonable and logical conclusion to the writer's argument.

Examiner's Comments

This is a very full answer which **covers all the bullet points** and is firmly **rooted in the text**. What is particularly impressive is the range of comment in the last paragraph about the **writer's different methods of persuasion** – explanations of **tone** and of how **sentence structures** are used will always gain high marks. This answer adopts a sensible approach by working chronologically through the text looking for fact and opinion, but then adopting a freer approach to language and methods of persuasion: this shows that the candidate **has taken in the whole text** and can move easily around it.

READING: Question 6

This final question is a large-scale comparison of two unseen texts on a similar theme. As is often the case in a task of this sort, you are given questions to answer on each text separately, and then a comparison. As in the previous sample question, you should use the initial task to help you prepare for the later, more demanding task. These answers are at Grade A. Compare your answers with them.

(a) (i) The reasons given are that young people may become homeless because they don't have a home provided for them by friends or family, or when they leave care; that they may be forced to leave home because of overcrowding or arguments, or because they have been abused or evicted; that they can't afford to get a home because they have no job, or their wages are too low; or that if they do have a home to begin with, they can't cope with housekeeping, especially budgeting, and so lose it.

(ii) The Children Act has not solved the problem because local authorities are too short of money to give help to homeless young people. The authorities also do not give enough advice to young people about how to manage their money if they are living alone, and they are often left to try and sort out their own accommodation in places they do not know or in lodgings which are only temporary.

Examiner's Comments

The answers on this first text are **complete and accurate**. Notice that more marks are available for (ii) than (i); this may have included too much for (i), but **as long as all the information is relevant** (which it is here) then it is never a bad idea to **give as full an answer as possible**.

(b) (i) The Salvation Army helps people like Jim by:

- providing them with hope and a fresh start
- building their confidence so that they are more likely to get a job
- providing temporary accommodation
- helping them find permanent homes
- providing sympathetic listeners
- providing friendship and care
- providing clothes and food
- providing comforts such as a bed and shaving materials.

(ii) (A) Words such as "prey" and "potential killers" shock the reader into realising how dangerous it is for homeless people on the streets and how they may be unable to prevent themselves becoming very ill or even dying.

(B) Mention of "Christmas" and "brighter" makes the reader realise what a difference the Salvation Army can make at a time of year when homeless people might feel very sad and alone. The second sentence is very short, and jolts you into realising that this affects real people.

(C) The use of "we" and the repetition of "the ones" makes it sound as though the Salvation Army can make a real difference to the support homeless people normally get.

Examiner's Comments

In the first part of this question, the candidate has sensibly assumed that 8 marks requires 8 points. There are more than 8 points in the passage, but there is no need to give them all – what the candidate has done is to select what appear to be the 8 **most significant** points. In the second part, there is a good **range of comments on different language features**, such as the impact of individual words and their associations, sentence structures and patterns. This shows that the candidate is aware of the **different levels at which a text can influence its readers**, and would gain high marks.

(c) These two leaflets are quite different, even though they are both about homelessness. The content of the first text is mostly concerned with surveys and legal processes to give a general, largely factual picture of the problem – both how it arises and what can or should be done to help improve the situation. The Salvation Army leaflet does contain some general information about the part the organisation plays in combating homelessness, but it also includes a case study of one person, Jim. The reader does not know whether Jim is a real person or not, but this technique makes the leaflet seem more personal and immediate than the first text, which comes across as "colder" or more "official".

This impression is reinforced by how the material is presented in both texts and by the nature of the language used. The first text is in standard newspaper format, with a headline, subheadings and columns. The sentences and paragraphs are fairly short and some bullet points are used to draw the reader's attention to main points at the start. The Salvation Army leaflet is similar in format, but includes a picture, and the subheadings are longer and more emotional than those in the first text. It also uses paragraphs in italics to emphasise main points in its message.

There is quite a difference in the language of the two texts. The vocabulary in the first text is chosen to give information, rather than to persuade, and the tone is consistent. The sentences are sometimes quite complex (for

example "Without work, … without a permanent address"). The Salvation Army leaflet mixes fact and opinion and makes an emotional appeal to readers through using everyday language (and sometimes slang – "I can't really blame the bloke at the hotel") to convey a moral story in simple sentences. There is a contrast between the style and tone of the passages about Jim and those about the work of the organisation, for example in the next-to-last paragraph which uses a long, repetitive sentence structure.

Examiner's Comments

This is another **full answer** which **covers the bullet points in the order suggested** and which examines each text in turn. Although you have not been asked to judge which text is the more successful, the candidate has **compared their features** and has related these to what it is they are trying to do. The answer therefore shows good **awareness of the importance of purpose and audience in evaluating texts**. The candidate has not used many quotations or references to illustrate the comments on language, but those chosen are sufficient.

WRITING: Question 1

In this question, you were given a fairly detailed plan to use. You should have followed its outline in terms of content, but you will have expressed your own views and feelings about the issues raised and you will have chosen your own order for dealing with them. You should have tried to introduce some material of your own. Compare your own answer with the one below (which would have gained an A). Read through the examiner's comments carefully.

Whether it is right or not to keep animals out of their natural surroundings has been a hot topic of debate for a long time. The debate probably began when early humans started to keep animals for food, or when they first introduced pets to the family cave, and it has raged ever since. I am going to explain my views on the subject by considering four aspects of this issue: keeping animals as pets, animals in zoos and circuses, farm animals and rearing animals for food, and the use of animals in medical research.

People like pets – that is, they like them if they're not terrified of them, or if they're not made ill by them. Those are serious matters: many people have phobias about all kinds of animals, and may stop visiting friends, or be afraid of calling on new acquaintances, if there is a possibility of coming face to face with their greatest fear. More seriously than this, perhaps, is the recent increase in the incidence of asthma in young children, much of it attributable to pet hairs. Other unpleasant diseases can be caught from parrots, and blindness can result from infections picked up from dog dirt. Young children are not naturally hygiene-conscious, and parents should think carefully before introducing pets into the home.

The problem of pets does not end in the home, either: sometimes dogs in particular are allowed to roam, or worse still are abandoned, so that stray animals and unwanted puppies have to be dealt with by local councils. Nobody likes the idea of putting animals down simply because they're an inconvenience, but this sadly has to be done sometimes if pet owners do not face up to their responsibilities.

The positive aspect of pets is, of course, the pleasure they give. Young children can learn to respect animals generally by loving their own pet, and lonely old people are often grateful for the companionship a pet can give. There are even cases where people in comas have been brought back to consciousness by hearing their dog bark, or by cuddling a cat. I have a pet cat, and would not be without it for the world. I think she likes living with me as much as I enjoy looking after her – but we can't really know that for certain, can we, and I do worry about pets which are neglected or ill-treated.

I have much firmer views on the subject of animals in zoos and circuses. It is wrong! There may be a case for sometimes keeping endangered species in safe, secure conditions so that they can breed and not become extinct, but that should be the only reason for keeping them in a zoo and they should be released back into the wild as soon as possible. The older I have become, the more I have grown to hate the idea of queuing up in zoos to stare at "cute" or "frightening" animals. It's not much better than going to laugh at the lunatics in eighteenth-century asylums, really. Circuses are even worse. At least modern zoos attempt to provide living conditions which are as natural as possible for the animals, but making them do humiliating "tricks" in circuses and keeping them in cages which are trundled around the country? Ugh! I don't agree that zoos are educational or that circuses are fun. Nowadays, it is easy enough to go and film animals in their natural surroundings for educational purposes. People who think it is harmless entertainment to watch performing animals in circuses are simply, to my mind, sick.

Now to the really big issue: animals as food! I cannot go into every aspect of this - it would take a lifetime. But I have some clear views of my own, although no doubt some people would find them unacceptable or contradictory. I believe that, in the end, most humans like to eat dairy products and meat. The issue then becomes not whether they should or not, but whether the animals providing these products are kept in decent conditions and whether they are killed humanely. I know that sounds blunt and perhaps uncomfortable, but it is what I believe. Many of my friends have become vegetarians, or even vegans, and I know that conditions on many farms or in abattoirs and food factories are not good. But that could be put right, and I do enjoy a good steak. That's all there is to it, really.

Finally, I come to the other hot topic: using animals in medical research. It is important to distinguish this from using animals to test cosmetics. Cosmetics are just a piece of human vanity and there is no justification at all for making animals suffer so that a teenager's spots can be better hidden. However, finding cures for diseases is another matter altogether, and my views on this are rather like those I have on eating meat: humans are more important than animals, and if there was a choice between someone in my family dying of cancer, or a cure being found which involved a few hundred mice and rabbits suffering, then I would not think twice about it.

You may find my views too forthright, but this is a complicated subject and if you don't have firm views you are likely to be indecisive about all aspects of it. In summary, I remain undecided about pets, but believe they probably do more good than harm. I disapprove totally of zoos and circuses. I am happy to eat meat and dairy products, but do not want animals to suffer unduly for it. Cosmetic research using animals is wrong, but medical research is necessary. So there you are: and perhaps it is a good thing that you are reading this, not hearing it from me face to face, as you may disagree violently!

Examiner's Comments

This **essay is introduced well**. Firstly, the candidate has set out the content and structure very clearly, using the given plan but re-arranged and added to in order to suit his/her own purposes. Secondly, there is a **humorous comment** at the start (*family cave*), and in the concluding paragraph, which lighten what could otherwise be an over-solemn piece of writing. This candidate has decided to **state his/her views firmly** rather than give a balanced argument, which is fine – as long as you can be sufficiently forceful (as here!).

The reader is addressed directly throughout, which adds to the impact, and there is lots of **evidence and anecdote to back up the points made** (for example about infant asthma and vegetarian friends). There is a **sophisticated range of vocabulary** (*incidence, attributable, humane*, etc.) and the **argument is clear and easily followed** thanks to **coherent sentencing and paragraphing**. Technically, the work is faultless – **grammar, spelling and punctuation all demonstrate high-order skills**. Even if an examiner disagreed with the views, the way they are presented would earn a very high mark indeed!

WRITING: Question 2

The following extracts provide an idea of how you might have started any one of the given descriptions. They are all of Grade A quality, so you can compare your own answers with them, once you have read through the examiner's comments.

A city at night

Car lights reflecting and flashing off the wet road; tyres swishing through the pools of standing water; young people out for the evening dodging the spray and giggling happily with their friends. That is the city most of you see, but I keep to the side streets and alleyways where I hope to find a dry, warm spot for the night. Here's an air vent from a restaurant: warm gusts of air laden with the aromas of spices from the exotic east … no dinner for me tonight, unless I'm lucky. Past a noisy backstreet pub now; everyone shouting – singing, maybe – and more lights and smells. Dustbin lids falling nearby; perhaps its another homeless person like me, or a cat on the prowl. I saw a fox once, vivid brown-red against a white shop wall, tearing a rubbish bag to pieces. Rubbish is everywhere. They put it out at night, great stacks of it waiting for the bin lorries which carry on their work all night long. They say the city never sleeps, and they're right …

Examiner's Comments

This description shows some **originality** by being written as if through the eyes of someone who sleeps rough in the city at night. This is fine, as long as you **don't get sidetracked away from the description** into telling a story. The writing uses some **interesting sentence structures**, for example the first one. The candidate has set up opportunities to show that s/he can use a **wide range of punctuation**, including the colon and semi-colon. The **choices of vocabulary are precise** and show that s/he has a variety of words on which to call.

A deserted beach

The water laps gently against the line of shingle which borders the wet sand, making a gentle sucking noise that seems to soothe away all the noise and strife of the day. Everyone has gone now; it is close to nightfall and the only noise apart from the waves is the distant call of gulls returning to their nesting-places. As darkness settles, the beach looks smooth, unruffled, rid of the hundreds of people who have trampled over it during the day. Some have left litter behind them, but in the gathering twilight even that becomes a series of exotic silhouettes against the western sky. The sky – luminous pink, then suddenly a deepening blue as the sun sinks further below the horizon and it becomes difficult to distinguish sand, shingle and sea any longer …

Examiner's Comments

As in the previous descriptive opening, the candidate has shown all the necessary skills to obtain a very high mark. There are **appropriate choices of vocabulary** and a **convincing atmosphere of calm**, as well as a **scene which is easy to picture in the reader's mind.** The choice of **onomatopoeic words** with many 's' sounds in the opening sentence is not original, but does evoke the sounds being described. Once again, **spelling and punctuation are faultless.**

A busy shopping centre

"Six peaches for a pound. Come on, love, you'll not find any better!"

"Robert! I'll not tell you again! Keep beside me or you'll be lost!"

"See you – when? What? I can't hear above all this row!"

Just a few of the calls, complaints and garbled arrangements being shouted out this thronging Saturday afternoon a few days before Christmas in the vast shopping centre which covers several hundred acres of what used to be countryside. Then, it was peaceful; now, from morning until night it is all hubbub, hurrying and hullabaloo. Fraught parents, demanding children, eager salespeople – they all contribute to the show of human frailties spread out for anyone to watch from the staircase balconies on the way to the rooftop car park. Worship of Mammon goes on here seven days a week, three hundred and sixty four days a year, better attended than any church in this modern age. Goods piled high everywhere, sometimes cheap, sometimes not, but all wanted by someone, somewhere – or so the frantic shoppers believe …

Examiner's Comments

This candidate has realised that **writing a description does not prevent the use of dialogue** to create atmosphere, to bring in some variety and contrast in styles of language and to show accurate use of speech marks! This piece shows a **very good use of contrasting styles**: different speech patterns, crafted sentences using alliteration and patterned structures (for example *Then … now*; *someone, somewhere*), and **a range of sophisticated vocabulary** (for example *fraught; Mammon*). **Technical accuracy is again faultless**, as it must be to gain the highest marks.

WRITING: Question 3

This sample answer, which would be awarded a Grade A, is a speech against the planned housing development. If you choose to answer a question of this type, it is often easier to write the 'anti' side: it gives you more scope for dramatic language! Compare your answer with this one and read through the examiner's comments carefully so that you understand what examiners are looking for in order to award high marks.

Fellow councillors, you won't be surprised to know that I'm speaking tonight against these ridiculous proposals to build houses and shops on Green Meadow. Over the years, we've seen more and more of the beautiful countryside which surrounds our town disappear beneath a sea of concrete and brick, and I say the time has come to shout, "Enough!"

What sort of future will our young children face if they have only small back gardens and busy streets to play in? How can they be safe from traffic? How can they learn to love the countryside and respect wildlife without any near at hand?

Already in our town we have houses standing empty because no-one will live in them. Yes, they may be old houses, lacking modern fittings, but we could invest the money in improving them rather than build new houses. Those old houses are near our Central Park, so there are play facilities for children close at hand, and more importantly, they're near the town centre shops. These shops are already struggling to stay in business because of the out-of-town shopping centre we approved five years ago – how much worse will it be for them if we now allow a huge new housing development on the other side of town, with its own local shops and a direct link to the hypermarket via the ring road?

Over the years we've given permission for all kinds of developments to go ahead in the name of progress. We haven't always stopped to think of the effects they might have on our historic town. Maybe it's time to stand back and look at what's worth preserving and improving, not what will make it seem that we're keeping up with all the other towns across the country.

We don't really want this town to look like anywhere else, do we? It certainly will if we give permission for this development. When visitors arrive by road now, most of them come past the edge of Green Meadow and it gives them a lovely view of the town across the rolling fields. It won't be quite the same if, minutes after they leave the motorway, they're in the middle of a housing estate with row upon row of identical houses.

And what about the history of Green Meadow? We all know that it was the site of a famous battle more than a thousand years ago in the days of the Viking invasions and that one day, when there are funds available, archaeologists from our university would like to excavate it for evidence of what took place. If they find important remains, it could really put our town on the tourist map. I know that not everyone is interested in history, but surely it can't be right to bury the site beneath this new development and deny any possibility of its ever being properly investigated.

I know that it will bring this council lots of money if we sell Green Meadow to a property developer. If we choose to modernise existing houses instead, that will cost us money. I know that sounds like a bad deal, and that we ought to earn money not spend it. With the income from the sale of Green Meadow we could carry out improvements to the town centre. But will there be a town centre worth improving for much longer if all the houses and all the business move to the outskirts?

Think about the longer term benefits. Think what future generations will say about our decision tonight. Think about the quality of life we want in our town.

I propose that we reject these plans. Thank you for listening to me.

Examiner's Comments

This is a **powerful and persuasive** speech. The **content is well-chosen**, but – more importantly – it has been made to sound like a speech by the style used. The **language is a good balance** between the **formal** (*I propose* … ; *longer term benefits*, etc.) and the **informal** (the use of contractions such as *can't*; phrases such as *a bad*

deal, etc.), and the candidate has very cleverly introduced the reference to the Viking battle to give a chance to show the correct spelling of the word *archaeologist*! This answer also shows an awareness that in speeches, **repetitive structures** are often used to have an almost hypnotic, persuasive effect on listeners – this technique is used in a number of places, for example the three questions in the second paragraph (and the use of **rhetorical questions** is a good device in itself) and in the last-but-one paragraph. The structure suits the purpose well, as the **paragraphs are short**, which makes the points easier for listeners to follow.

WRITING: Question 4

Your own story is unlikely to resemble at all the one that follows! This one would be awarded a Grade A. The comments made at the end of it should help you to assess your own writing and to decide whether it demonstrates the skills needed for it to be awarded a similarly high mark.

It was a cold winter's night. Gusting winds, driving rain and dropping temperatures meant that I was glad to be indoors. One of my favourite programmes was on the television, the fire was roaring up the chimney, my annoying little sister was staying at her friend's for the night and I felt snug and happy. All that could go wrong would be my older brother coming in before I went to bed. There would be a row between him and my mum, as there always was. She felt he was out of control since dad had left – "Thinks he's the big man of the house now, and has to throw his weight around like his father before him", as she used to complain bitterly whenever he gave her the slightest opening.

Don't get me wrong: I love my family, but like all families – and more than some – we have our tensions, and it's just nice to be alone now and then. Well, almost alone. Mum was in, of course; she's never out any more – but in a funny kind of way she's never in, either. She just seems sort of vacant, distant, as though dad finally going knocked all the life out of her.

The door banged and Paul lumbered into the room. He's a big lad, naturally clumsy, but he'd obviously been drinking with his college friends. As he swung heavily towards the sofa his arm caught a vase which was on a table beside the fireplace, and it smashed into dozens of pieces on the tiled hearth. It was an ugly old thing, but I knew mum liked it for some reason and I knew that breaking it meant trouble for Paul and an end to my peaceful evening.

I made my mind up in a flash, leapt to my feet, and before mum had even rushed into the room to look at the mess I was already mumbling, "Sorry, mum, I just sort of overbalanced". Paul looked at me astonished, but said nothing. Mum was ominously quiet, then the storm broke. She cried. She shouted. She came so close to me with her face jutting into mine that I thought she was going to hit me for the first time since I was a small child. I couldn't believe how cruel some of the things were that she said - it was only a rotten vase, after all, and I had taken the blame to stop a shouting match like this with Paul.

Paul – of course, he said nothing. He probably realised that if I was getting this treatment, he'd get something even worse if he owned up, and anyway the situation was past the point of no return. We couldn't tell the truth without making the whole business even worse. The thing is, I was able to piece together the story from the apparently incoherent scraps she yelled at me. It turned out the vase had been given to her as a wedding present, more than twenty years ago, by someone who had been her boyfriend before she met dad and who she now regretted not having stuck with. She'd never told dad where it came from, but even from the start of her marriage this vase had become a kind of symbol of what might have been, a reminder of someone who could have given her a better life.

Now she had got it into her head that I had known all of this, goodness knows how, and that "daddy's little princess", as she venomously called me, had decided to get at her by smashing it. I tried to tell her she'd got it all wrong. At last I appealed to Paul but he ignored me and then she began to scream at me even more for trying to blame my brother and avoid my responsibilities. Suddenly, and ridiculously, he was the blue-eyed boy and I was the one who had caused all the unhappiness in the family because I couldn't see dad in his true light and had tried to keep the peace between my parents in the past.

Then, as it always did, the hurricane subsided. She sat down and started crying. I tried to put an arm round her and tell her it was all right, but she pushed me away. Paul looked at me and grinned. No word of thanks, sympathy or anything.

It was all normal again the next day – as normal as anything ever could be in that bitter house. But I knew my mother. This would be held against me: she knew I had broken the vase on purpose, no matter what anyone said, and it would be used against me just as she used Paul's clumsiness against him.

It was so unfair. I know she can't help it really, but it-is-so-unfair.

Examiner's Comments

This story is a **well-planned narrative** which uses a **good range of vocabulary and varied sentence structures**. It has avoided the trap of trying to pack too much incident into a short space and has concentrated instead on a **straightforward situation** which causes conflict between the characters involved. This has allowed the candidate to include some **direct speech** and to **describe people who react differently** to what happens. By taking the reader into her thoughts **this answer successfully engages and sustains the reader's interest in, and sympathy for, the main character.**

Technically, the piece of **writing is very accurate**: it has **used a range of punctuation accurately**, **spellings are all correct**, and **paragraphs are used to structure the narrative helpfully**. The ending shows effective use of a short paragraph and a conscious tense change which, together with the hyphens between the last four words, is an **extremely powerful way of suggesting how this incident in the past still weighs on the narrator's mind.**

In order to perform at your best in the exam, you need to be in control of your whole approach to it. There are many ways you can prepare beforehand, and a range of simple techniques you can follow when you are answering actual questions during the exam.

Before the exam

Preparing pre-release materials

The Exam Board will usually provide an introduction and/or brief notes which tell you something about the texts and their authors.

Read this pre-release material carefully, as it will:
- provide you with information about texts and authors to help you understand them better
- relate different texts to one another and so help you to think about comparisons
- prepare you for the kinds of questions you may be asked in the exam.

Many Exam Boards allow you to annotate the material briefly, so take advantage of this by:
- writing the meanings of words or phrases in the margin
- underlining or highlighting words and phrases which may be good to refer to in your answer
- cross-referencing details from one text to another.

Remember not to write lots of irrelevant background information on the material – the examiner will want to see how you respond to the texts, not how much general knowledge you have.

Do not write pre-prepared answers on the material – this is cheating, and may get you disqualified. In any case, you must answer the actual questions on the exam paper, not the ones you would like to answer because you have practised them beforehand!

Decide what you understand and like (or dislike) about each text and think about different ways of reading them, so that you can write about alternative interpretations.

Make separate revision notes under these headings:
- text(s) I enjoyed or did not enjoy, and why
- thematic connections between texts
- interesting or unusual uses of language in texts
- interesting or unusual ideas in texts
- interesting or unusual writing techniques, devices or structures
- main points of interest in character, setting or theme
- similarities and differences between texts – themes, ideas, techniques, purpose, audience, language, etc.

Other preparation

There are a number of useful documents you can study. If your teacher does not provide them, or if you are preparing for the exam by yourself, contact your examination group for details of how to obtain them.

- Read Chief Examiners' reports on previous exams: these tell you why answers succeed or fail generally, and the common mistakes candidates make.
- Study mark schemes for past papers: these tell you how marks are gained in specific types of questions.
- Look at the kinds of questions you are likely to face by studying past papers: you are then less likely to be surprised in the exam.
- Make sure that you know the latest syllabus requirements: again, this will prevent any nasty surprises in the exam.

Practise writing to the time limits of the exam, ensuring that you can write neatly and accurately at speed.

In the exam

Read all instructions on the paper carefully so that you can:

- be sure about how many questions you have to answer overall, whether some need to come from certain sections, whether there are choices within questions, etc.
- work out how long to spend on each question. To do this effectively, you must allocate time to each question in relation to the marks it carries – in other words, spend twice as long on a question worth 10 marks as on one worth only 5 marks
- check which text(s) or part(s) of text(s) you need to use in answering Reading questions
- check whether Writing questions require you to use your own knowledge and/or imagination or whether you can use some of the reading text on the paper for ideas.

Questions on Reading

If there are only a few questions on the paper, it is a good idea to read the questions before you read the texts so that you know what you are looking for – in other words, you will be reading with a purpose. When you look at each question, make sure that you:

- look at key words so that you understand exactly what you are required to do. It can be a good idea to underline or highlight them so that you remember to focus on them in your answer
- take note of any advice about the structure or form of your answer. For example, there may be a series of bullet points or headings to follow.

As you read each piece of text, think (and, if you like, make brief notes) about your first reactions to:

- events, settings, characters or ideas in fiction and poetry texts
- information, facts and opinions in non-fiction texts
- any ideas, concerns or attitudes that seem interesting, or different, or difficult
- the language, techniques and presentation used by the writers.

Plan your answer in note or outline form, to make sure that you:

- don't rush into answers before you have thought through all that you want to say
- can think about the overall shape and logic of your answer
- choose the best references to, and quotations from, the text.

Check your answer, to make sure that you have:

- expressed yourself clearly
- used accurate spelling, punctuation and grammar
- included all the relevant material
- used sufficient references and quotations
- kept the question in focus.

Avoiding common mistakes

Remember to:

- comment and analyse, don't just describe – think **how** and **why** rather than **what**
- use quotation selectively, not just everything you can think of
- analyse specific details of language and presentation, rather than making vague generalisations.

Questions on Writing

General hints

In any kind of writing under exam conditions, make sure that you:

- understand how to use stimulus material if it is provided
- make an outline paragraph plan to help you structure the whole answer
- draft opening and closing paragraphs in some detail to ensure they are effective
- write at your normal speed, taking care over accuracy and legibility
- keep thinking about purpose and audience – are you presenting the right kind of material in the right kind of way?

Writing tasks to explore, imagine, entertain

You need to:

- decide on the ideas, feelings and situations that you want to explore in your writing
- imagine the sort of behaviour, dialogue, reactions and settings that will make your characters or situations believable
- remember that to entertain does not necessarily mean humour: suspense, surprise and conflict may be appropriate, depending on the content of your writing.

Writing tasks to inform, explain, describe

You need to:

- think purpose – what is the point of the information, explanation or description you are writing?
- think audience – how will this affect the content, tone and style of your writing?
- think response – do you want your reader to feel challenged, amused, reassured, flattered? Your choice of language needs to reflect this.

Writing tasks to argue, persuade, instruct

You need to:

- think about the viewpoint you adopt – is it to be a powerful one-sided statement or a rational consideration of different opinions?
- think about the language you use – will it achieve most by shock tactics, or by being cool and reasoned?
- think about the evidence you can use to support your case and affect the reader's response.

Writing tasks to analyse, review, comment

You need to:

- convey the special qualities of whatever you are writing about by analysing what effect it has on you, and why
- examine the evidence, weighing one aspect against another, so that you review the subject thoroughly
- summarise your thoughts and feelings through precisely expressed comments.

Avoiding common mistakes

Remember to:

- keep to the subject – don't twist a question to fit something you had prepared earlier
- keep narratives simple and explanations relevant and logical
- make sure your tone is appropriate – never forget the audience
- use a wide range of vocabulary and grammatical constructions – don't be afraid of making occasional mistakes as this is better than using a simple, restricted style of writing.